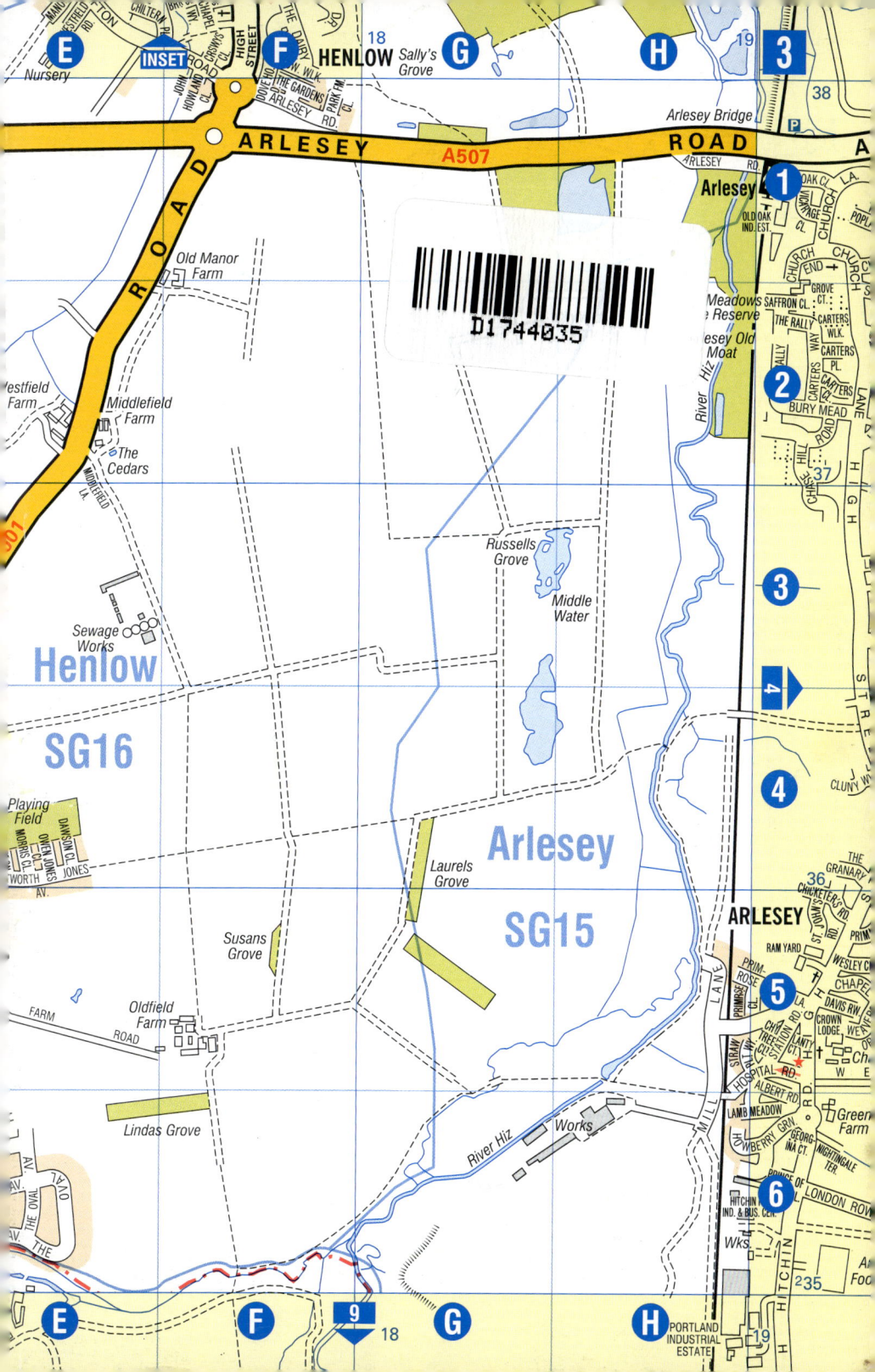

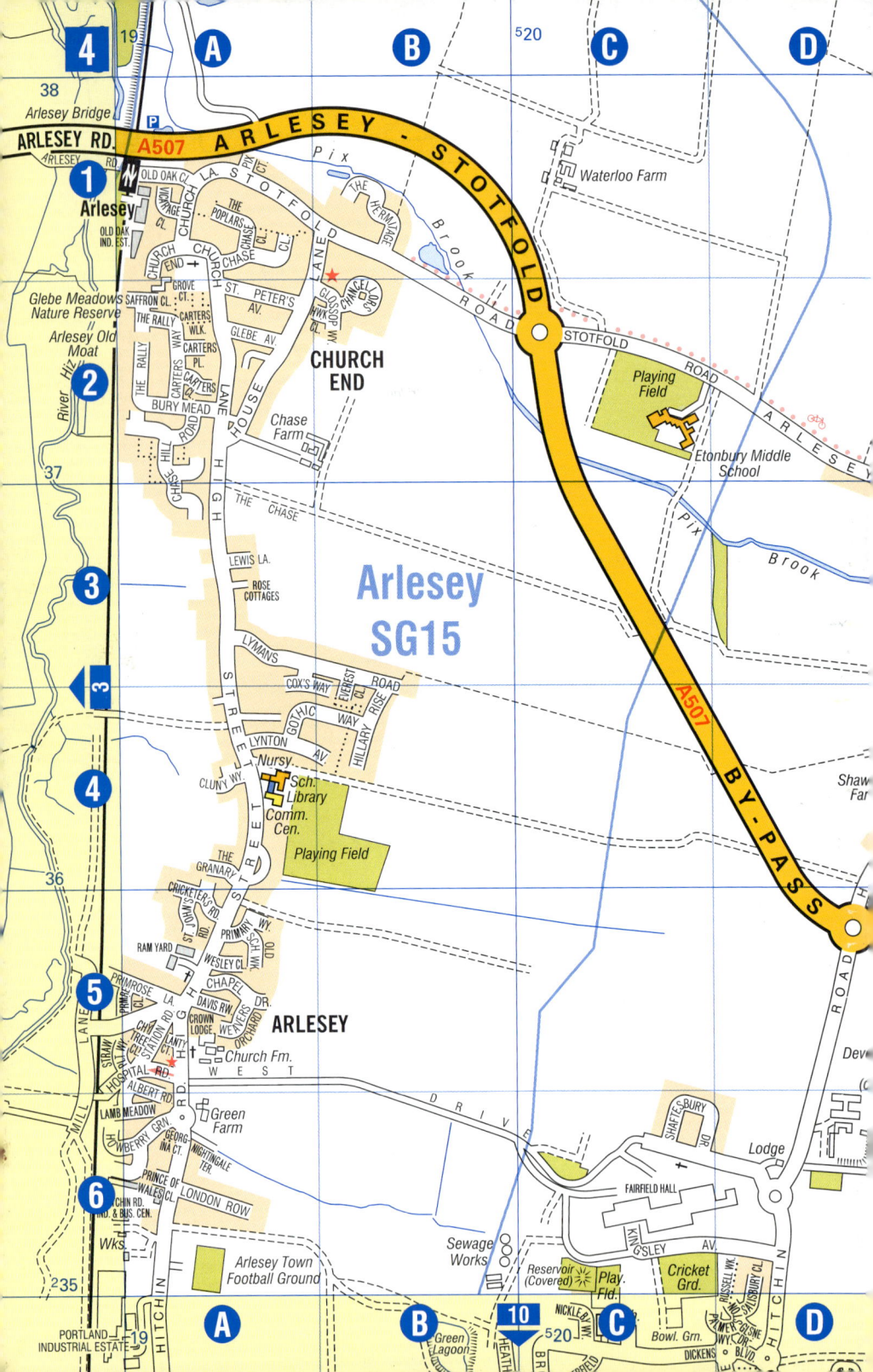

A-Z STEVENAGE

CONTENTS

REFERENCE

Motorway	**A1(M)**
A Road	**A602**
B Road	**B656**
Dual Carriageway	
One-way Street	
Traffic flow on A Roads is also indicated by a heavy line on the driver's left.	
Restricted Access	
Pedestrianized Road	
Residential Walkway	
Track / Footpath	
Local Authority Boundary	
Posttown Boundary	
Postcode Boundary (within Posttown)	
Railway	Station
Built-up Area	
Map Continuation	10
Car Park Selected	P

Church or Chapel	†
Cycle Route	
Fire Station	■
Hospital	H
House Numbers A & B Roads only	94 11
Information Centre	i
National Grid Reference	525
Police Station	▲
Post Office	★
Safety Camera with Speed Limit	30
Fixed cameras and long term road work cameras Symbols do not indicate camera direction	
Toilet	
without facilities for the Disabled	▽
with facilities for the Disabled	▽
Educational Establishment	
Hospital or Healthcare Building	
Industrial Building	
Leisure or Recreational Facility	
Place of Interest	
Public Building	
Shopping Centre or Market	
Other Selected Buildings	

Scale

1:15840   4 inches to 1 mile
6.31 cm to 1 km   10.16 cm to 1 mile

0   ¼   ½ Mile

0   250   500   750 Metres   1 Kilometre

Copyright of Geographers' A-Z Map Company Limited

Fairfield Road, Borough Green, Sevenoaks, Kent TN15 8PP
Telephone: 01732 781000 (Enquiries & Trade Sales)
01732 783422 (Retail Sales)

www.a-zmaps.co.uk

Copyright © Geographers' A-Z Map Co. Ltd.

Edition 3 2009

Ordnance Survey

This product includes mapping data licensed from Ordnance Survey® with the permission of the Controller of Her Majesty's Stationery Office.

© Crown Copyright 2008. All rights reserved. Licence number 100017302

Safety camera information supplied by www.PocketGPSWorld.com
Speed Camera Location Database Copyright 2008 © PocketGPSWorld.com

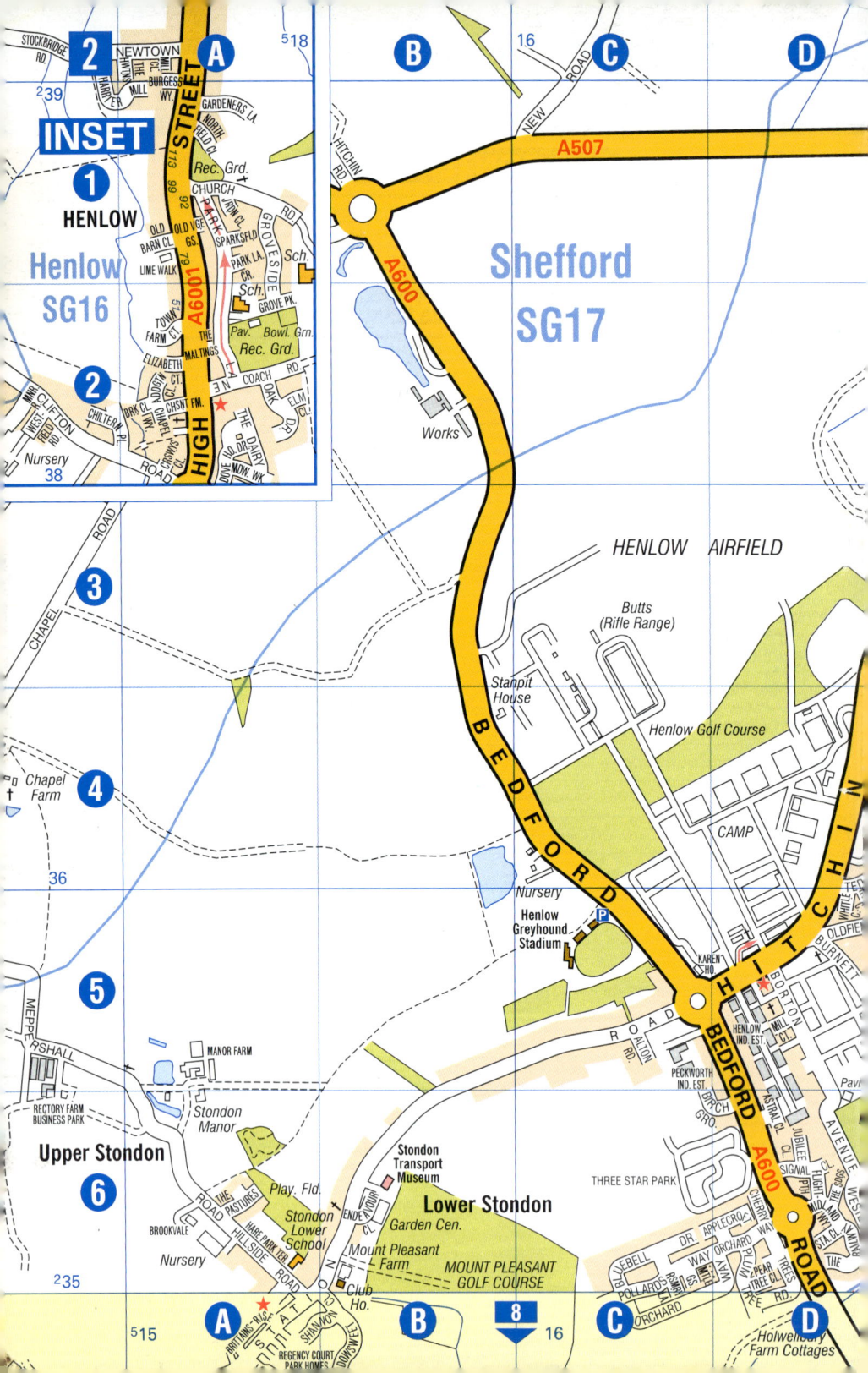

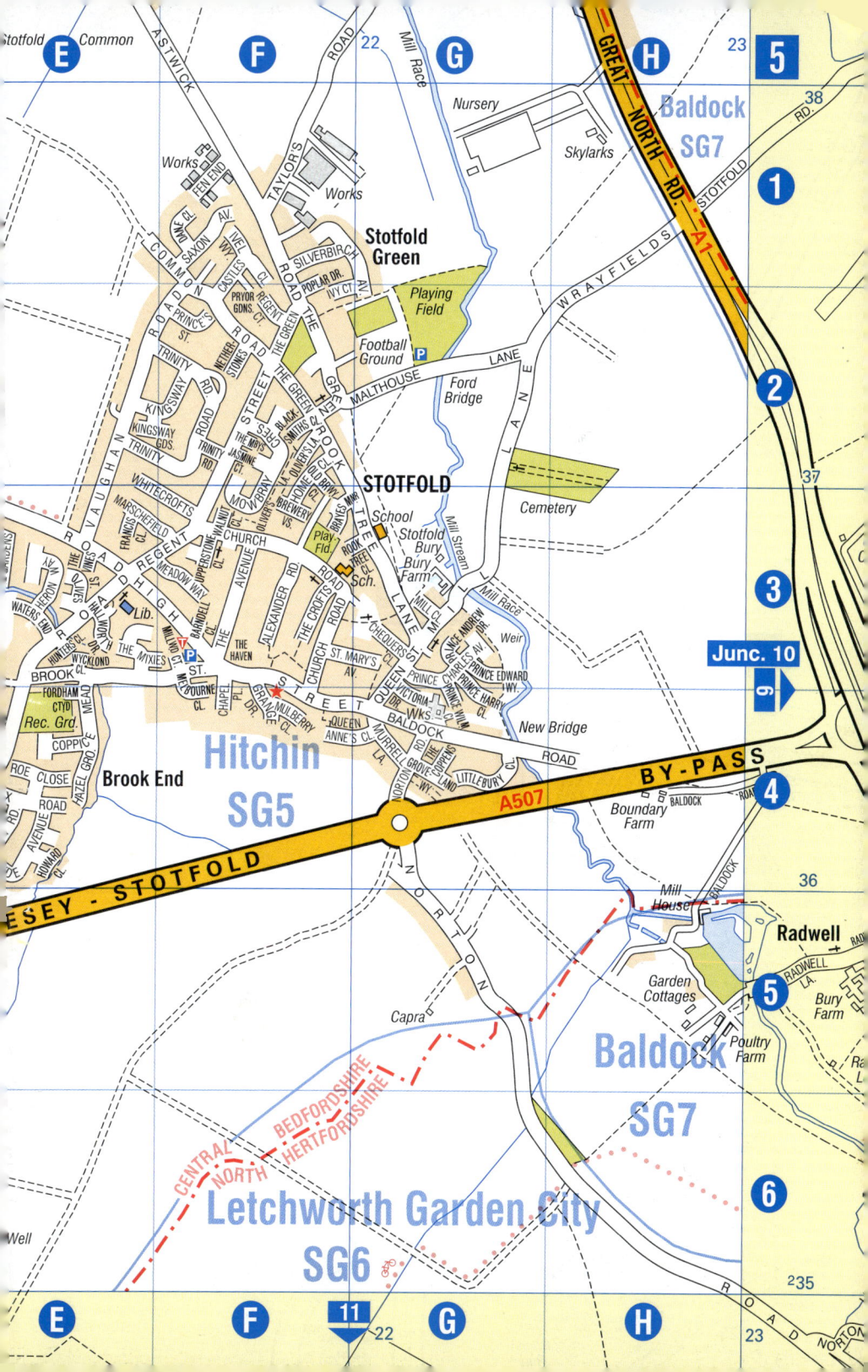

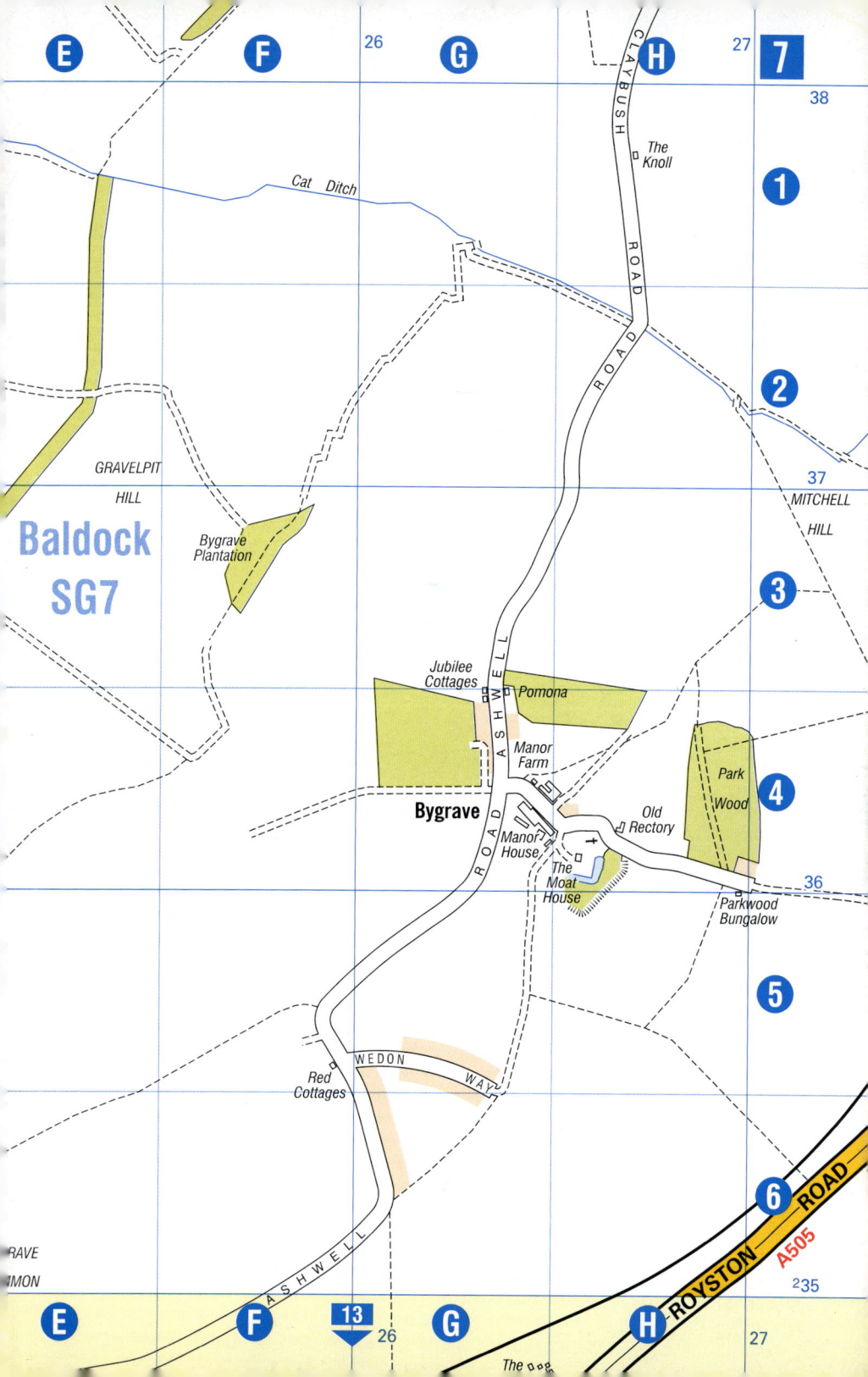

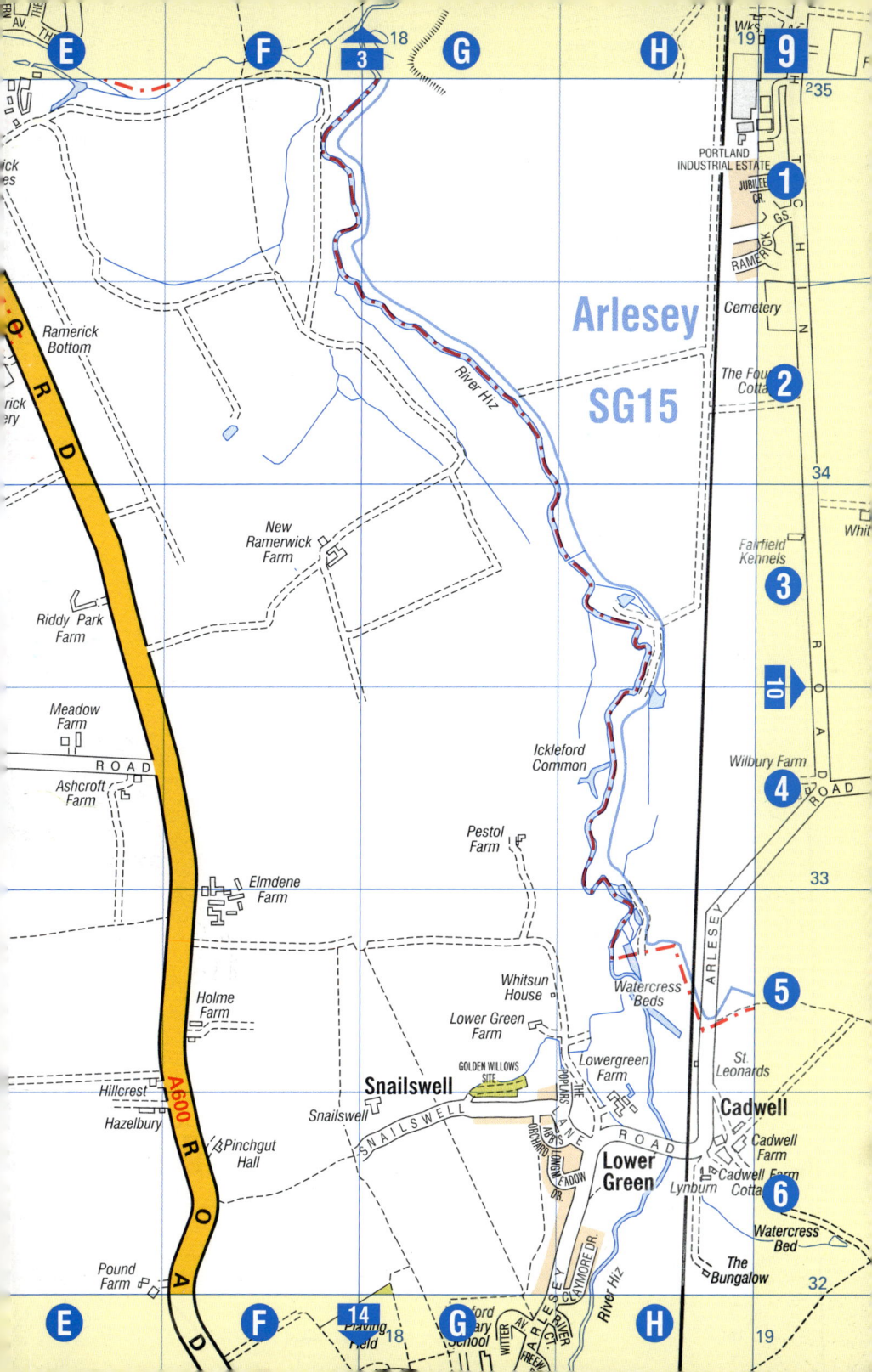

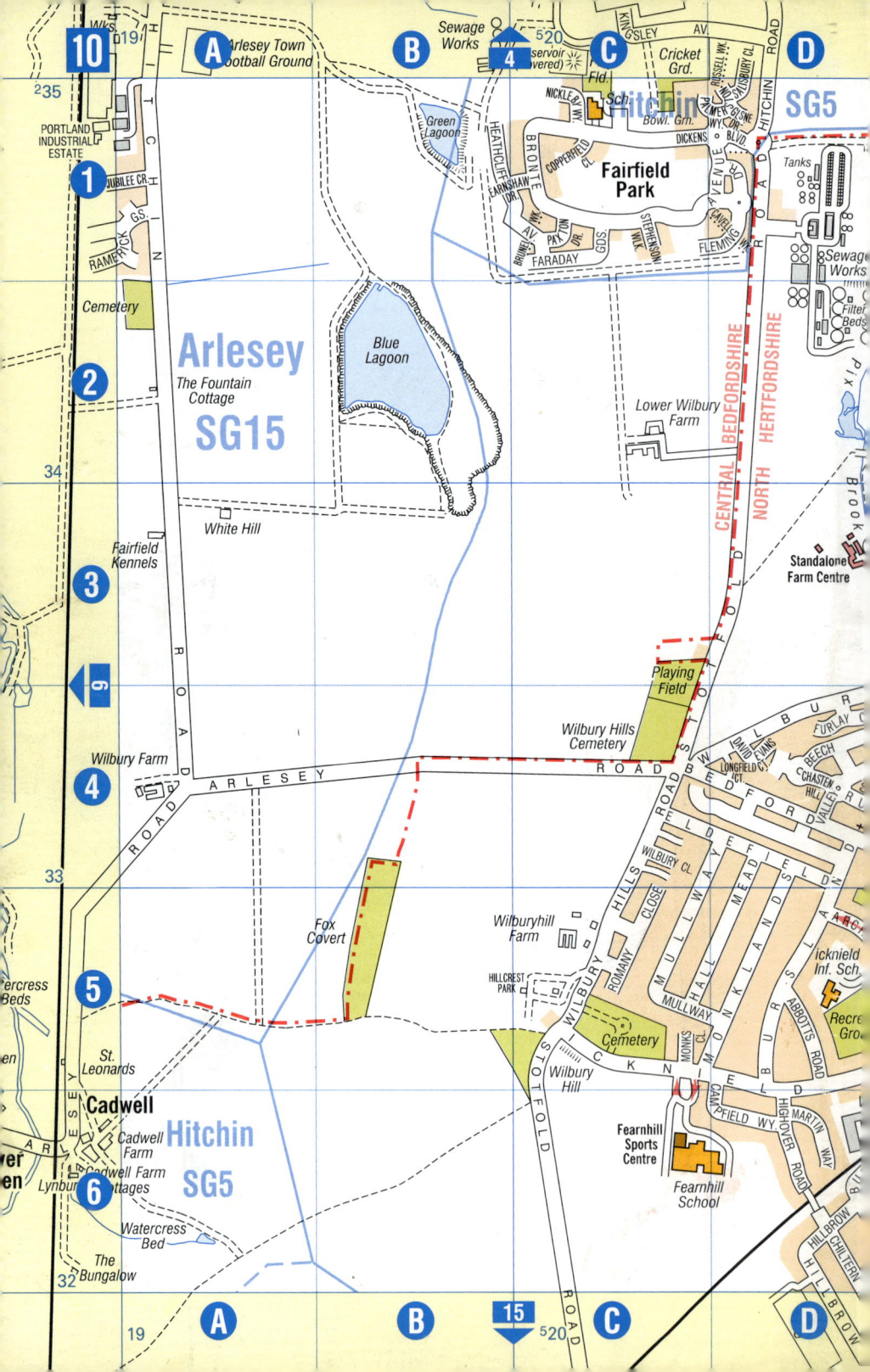

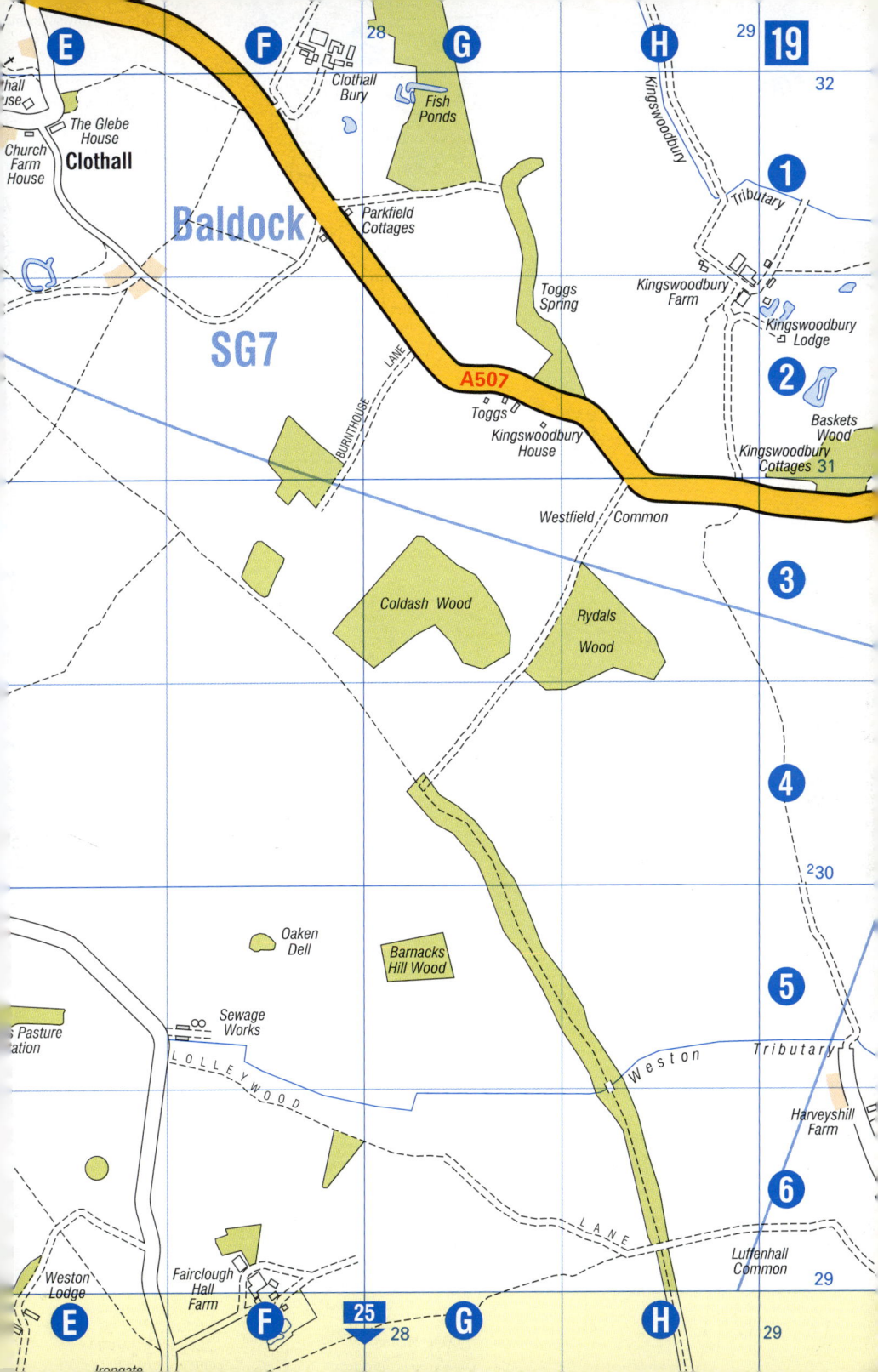

The Glebe House

Church Farm House

Clothall

Baldock

Clothall Bury

Fish Ponds

1

Parkfield Cottages

Kingswoodbury Farm

Kingswoodbury Lodge

Toggs Spring

SG7

BURNTHOUSE LANE

A507

Toggs

Kingswoodbury House

Baskets Wood

Kingswoodbury Cottages   31

2

Westfield   Common

3

Coldash   Wood

Rydals Wood

4

²30

Oaken Dell

Barnacks Hill Wood

5

Pasture ation

Sewage Works

LOLLEYWOOD

Weston   Tributary

Harveyshill Farm

6

Weston Lodge

Fairclough Hall Farm

LANE

Luffenhall Common   29

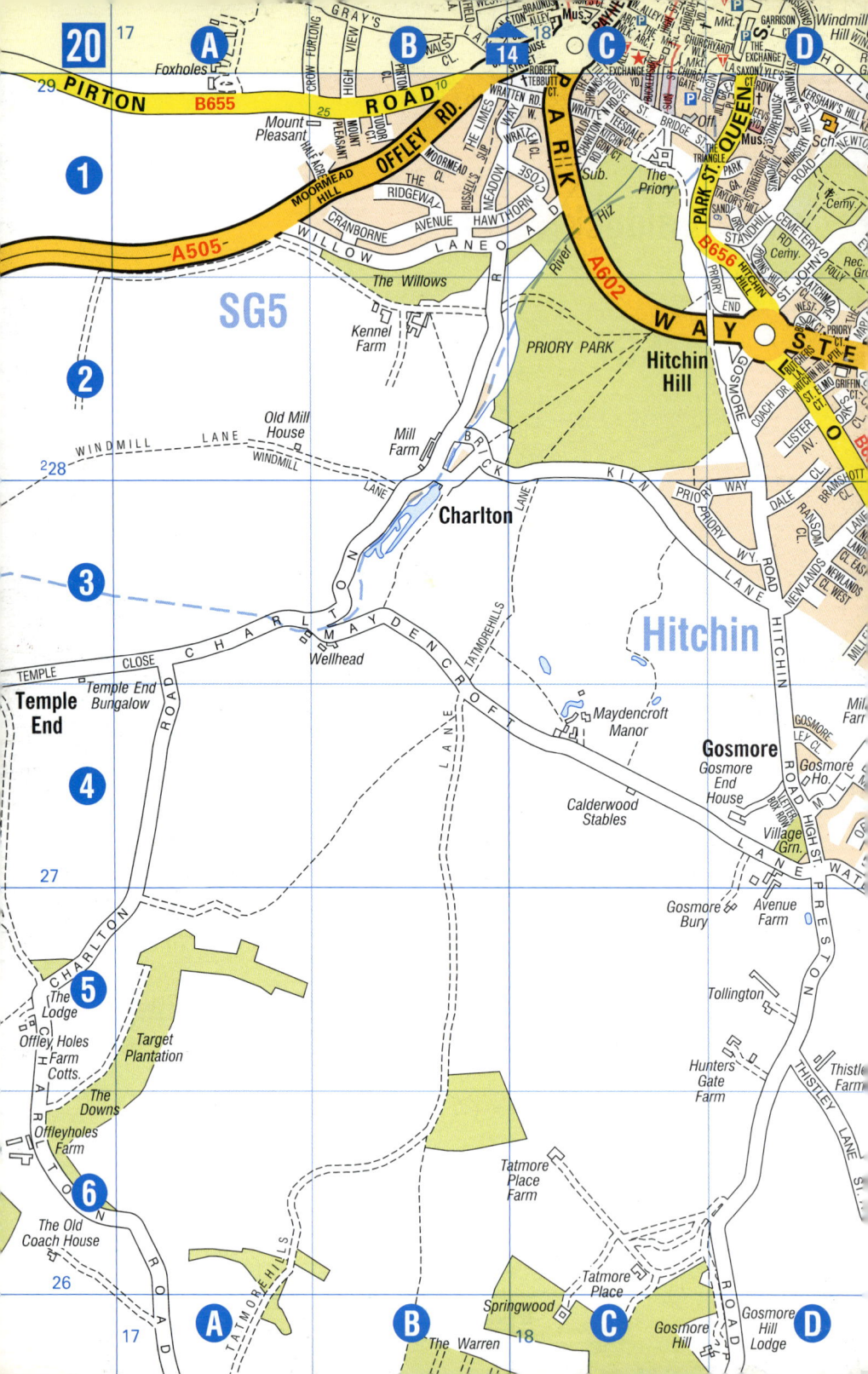

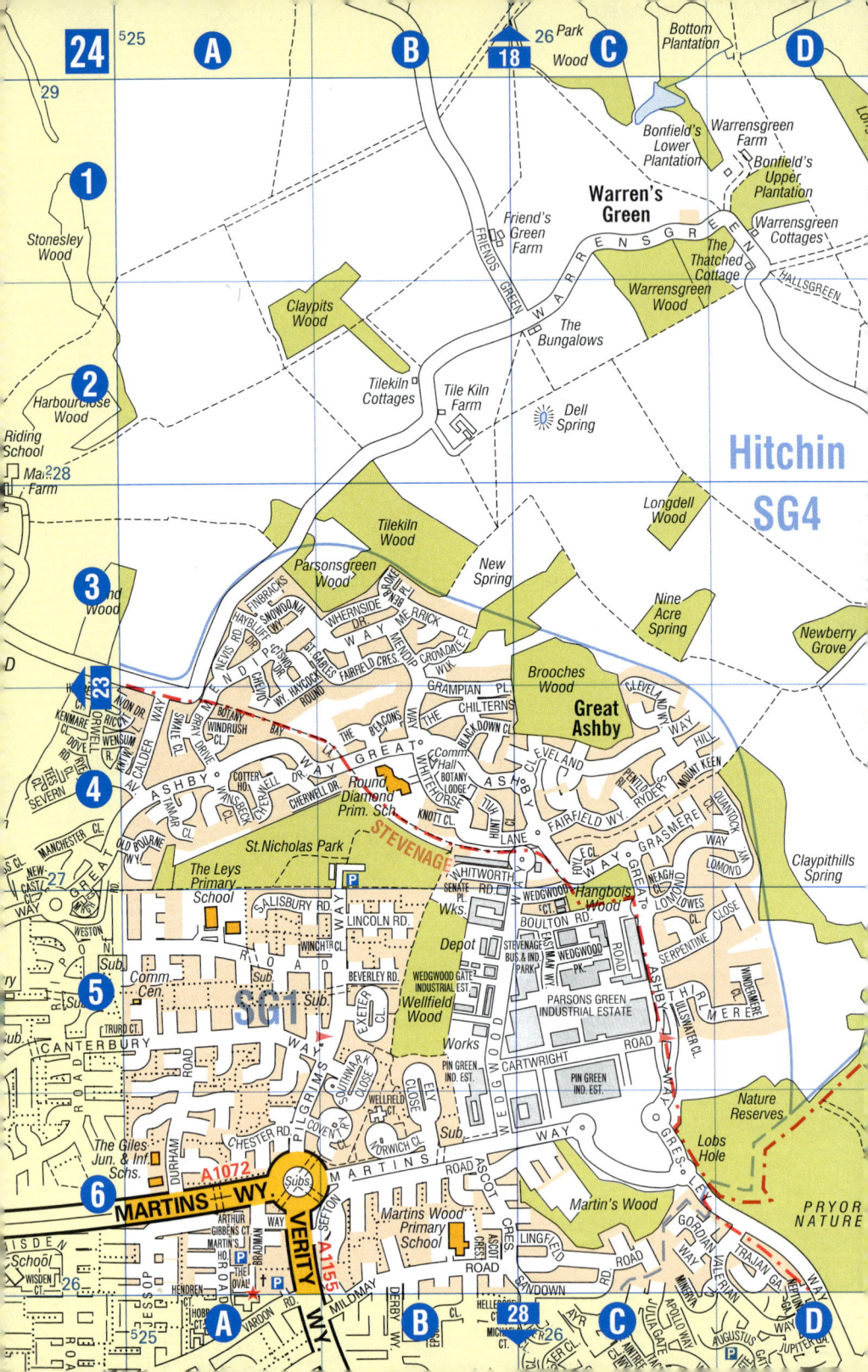

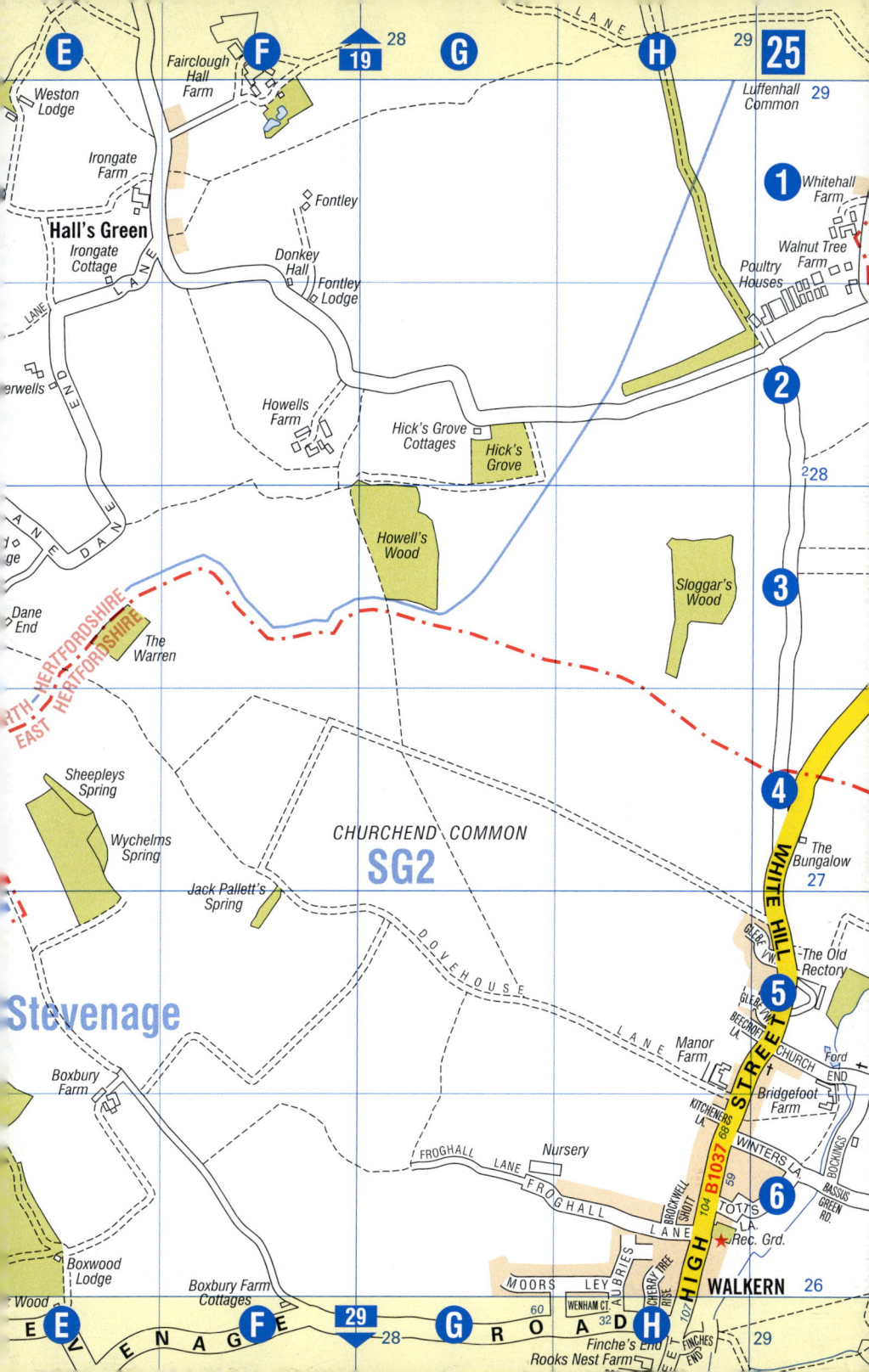

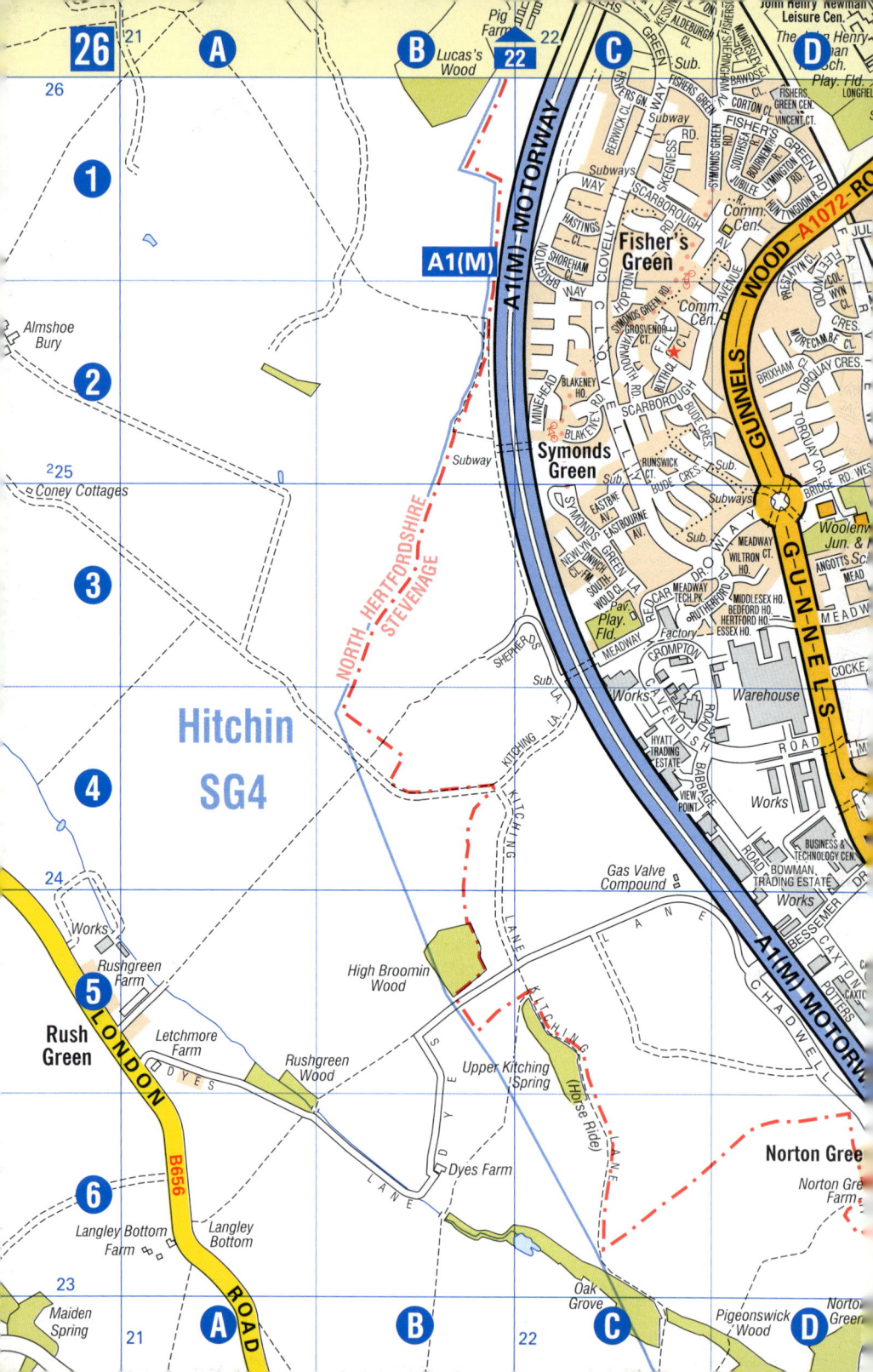

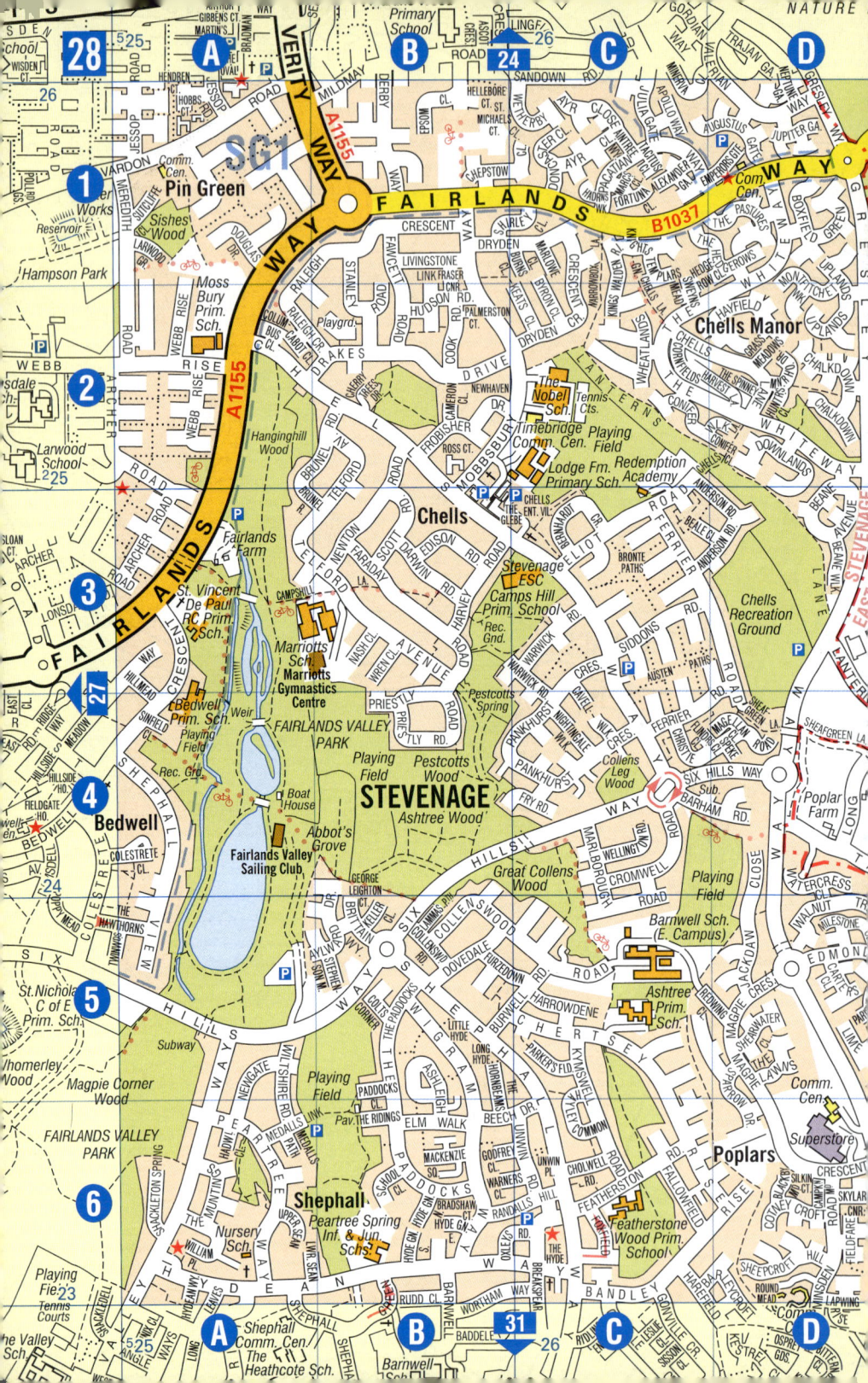

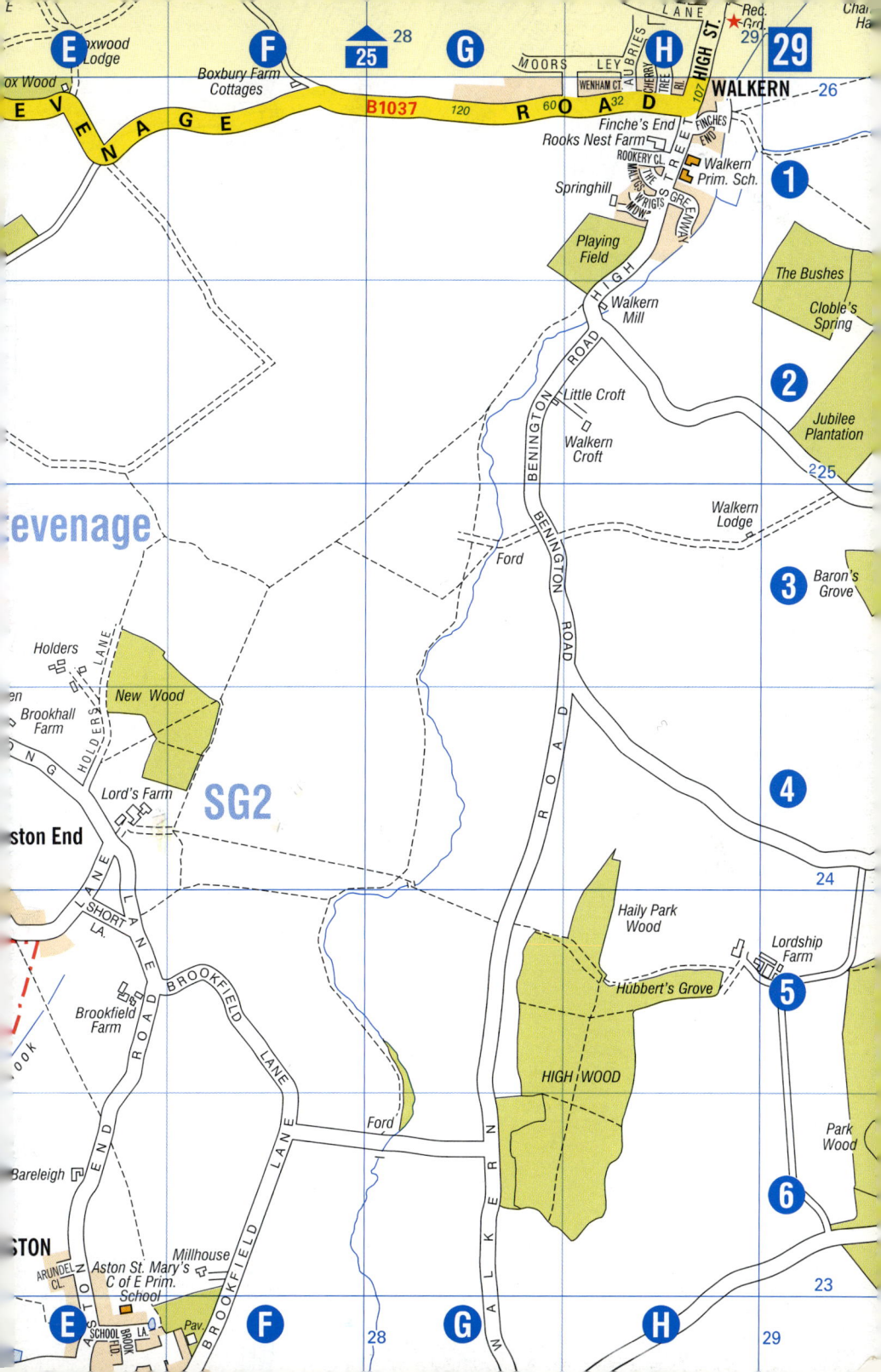

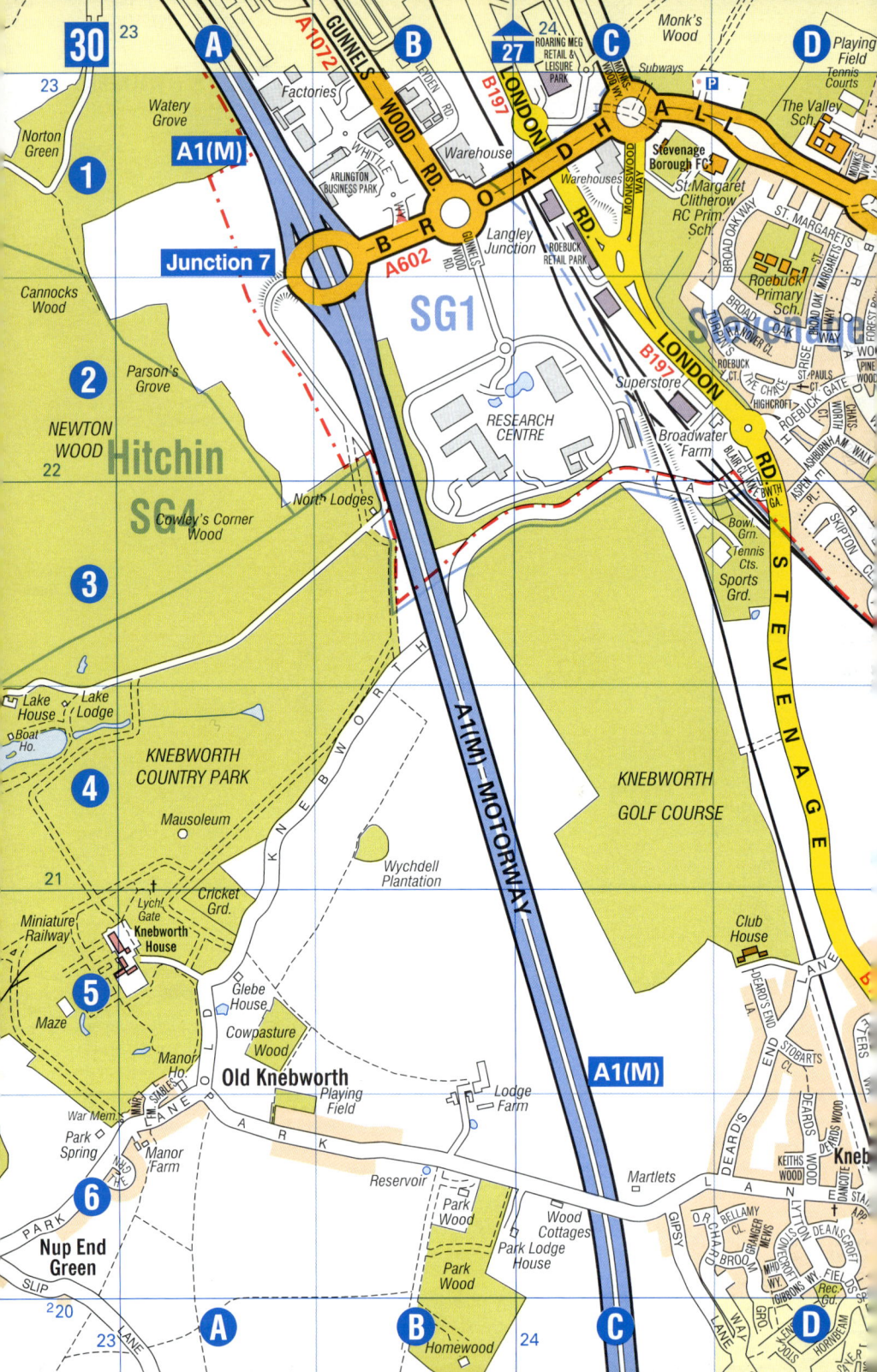

INDEX

Including Streets, Places & Areas, Hospitals etc., Industrial Estates,
Selected Flats & Walkways, Service Areas, Stations and Selected Places of Interest.

HOW TO USE THIS INDEX

1. Each street name is followed by its Postcode District, then by its Locality abbreviation(s) and then by its map reference:
   e.g. **Aleyn Way** SG7: Bald . . . .2F **13** is in the SG7 Postcode District and the Baldock Locality and is to be found in square 2F on page **13**.
   The page number is shown in bold type.

2. A strict alphabetical order is followed in which Av., Rd., St., etc. (though abbreviated) are read in full and as part of the street name;
   e.g. **Ash Dr.** appears after **Ashdown Rd.** but before **Ashleigh**

3. Streets and a selection of flats and walkways too small to be shown on the maps, appear in the index with the thoroughfare to which it is connected shown
   in brackets; e.g. **Appletrees** SG5: Hit . . . .1C **20** (off Wratten Rd. W.)

4. Addresses that are in more than one part are referred to as not continuous.

5. Places and areas are shown in the index in BLUE TYPE and the map reference is to the actual map square in which the town centre or area is located and
   not to the place name shown on the map; e.g. BALDOCK 3D **12**

6. An example of a selected place of interest is British Schools Mus. 1D **20**

7. An example of a station is Arlesey Station (Rail) 1A **4**

8. Service Areas are shown in the index in BOLD CAPITAL TYPE; e.g. BALDOCK SERVICE AREA 3B **6**

9. An example of a hospital or hospice is ERNEST GARDINER DAY HOSPITAL 6H **11**

GENERAL ABBREVIATIONS

All. : Alley	**Cres.** : Crescent	**Ho.** : House	**Pl.** : Place
App. : Approach	**Cft.** : Croft	**Ind.** : Industrial	**Ri.** : Rise
Av. : Avenue	**Dr.** : Drive	**Info.** : Information	**Rd.** : Road
Blvd. : Boulevard	**E.** : East	**La.** : Lane	**Shop.** : Shopping
Bri. : Bridge	**Ent.** : Enterprise	**Lit.** : Little	**Sth.** : South
Bus. : Business	**Est.** : Estate	**Mnr.** : Manor	**Sq.** : Square
Cen. : Centre	**Fld.** : Field	**Mdw.** : Meadow	**St.** : Street
Chu. : Church	**Flds.** : Fields	**Mdws.** : Meadows	**Ter.** : Terrace
Cl. : Close	**Gdns.** : Gardens	**M.** : Mews	**Trad.** : Trading
Comn. : Common	**Gth.** : Garth	**Mt.** : Mount	**Up.** : Upper
Cnr. : Corner	**Ga.** : Gate	**Mus.** : Museum	**Vw.** : View
Cott. : Cottage	**Gt.** : Great	**Nth.** : North	**Wlk.** : Walk
Cotts. : Cottages	**Grn.** : Green	**Pde.** : Parade	**W.** : West
Ct. : Court	**Gro.** : Grove	**Pk.** : Park	**Yd.** : Yard

LOCALITY ABBREVIATIONS

Arl : **Arlesey**	Dat : **Datchworth**	L Gar : **Letchworth Garden City**	Shef : **Shefford**
Ashw : **Ashwell**	Gos : **Gosmore**	L Wym : **Little Wymondley**	Stev : **Stevenage**
A'ton : **Aston**	G'ley : **Graveley**	L Ston : **Lower Stondon**	Stot : **Stotfold**
Ast E : **Aston End**	Gt Wym : **Great Wymondsley**	Mepp : **Meppershall**	U Sto : **Upper Stondon**
Astw : **Astwick**	H'low : **Henlow**	New : **Newnham**	Walk : **Walkern**
Bald : **Baldock**	Hinx : **Hinxworth**	Nort : **Norton**	Wall : **Wallington**
Byg : **Bygrave**	Hit : **Hitchin**	Old K : **Old Knebworth**	West : **Weston**
Cald : **Caldecote**	Hol : **Holwell**	Pirt : **Pirton**	Will : **Willan**
C'ton : **Charlton**	Ick : **Ickleford**	Pres : **Preston**	
Clift : **Clifton**	Kneb : **Knebworth**	R'well : **Radwell**	
Clo : **Clothall**	Lang : **Langley**	St Ipo : **St Ippollitts**	

A

	Alton Rd. SG16: L Ston 5C 2	**ARLESEY** **5A 4**
	Amor Way SG6: L Gar 5H 11	Arlesey Ho. SG15: Arl 1A 4
	Anchor Rd. SG7: Bald 4D 12	(off Church End)
Abbis Orchard SG5: Ick 6G 9	Anderson Rd. SG2: Stev 3D 28	Arlesey Rd. SG5: Ick 2C 14
Abbots Gro. SG1: Stev 5H 27	Andersons Ho. SG5: Hit 5D 14	SG5: Stot 2D 4
Abbotts Rd. SG6: L Gar 5D 10	Angle Ways SG2: Stev 1E 31	SG6: L Gar 4A 10
Abinger Cl. SG1: Stev 6G 27	Angotts Mead SG1: Stev 3D 26	SG15: Arl 5H 9
Acre Piece SG4: Hit 1E 21	Ansell Ct. SG1: Stev 6D 22	SG16: H'low 1F 3
Addington Cl. SG16: H'low 2A 2	Apollo Way SG2: Stev 1C 28	Arlesey Station (Rail) 1A 4
Aintree Way SG1: Stev 1C 28	Applecroft SG16: L Ston 6D 2	Arlesey-Stotfold By-Pass
Alban Rd. SG6: L Gar 2E 17	Appletrees SG5: Hit 1C 20	SG5: Stot 5E 5
Albert Rd. SG15: Arl 5A 4	(off Wratten Rd. W.)	SG15: Arl 1A 4
Albert St. SG1: Stev 2E 27	Arcade, The SG5: Hit 6C 14	Arlington Bus. Pk.
Aldeburgh Cl. SG1: Stev 6C 22	SG6: L Gar 5F 11	SG1: Stev 1B 30
Alder Cl. SG7: Bald 4C 12	Arcade Wlk. SG5: Hit 6C 14	Armour Ri. SG4: Hit 3F 15
Aldock Rd. SG1: Stev 2G 27	Archer Rd. SG1: Stev 3H 27	Arnold Cl. SG1: Stev 5F 23
Aldridge Ct. SG7: Bald 2C 12	Archers Way SG6: L Gar 6D 10	CC4: Hit 5F 15
Alexander Ga. SG1: Stev 1C 28	Arches, The SG6: L Gar 4G 11	Arthur Gibbens Ct.
Alexander Rd. SG5: Stot 3F 5	Arch Rd. SG4: Gt Wym 3H 21	SG1: Stev 6A 24
Alexandra Rd. SG5: Hit 4D 14	Arden Press Way	Arundel Cl. SG2: A'ton 6E 29
Aleyn Way SG7: Bald 2F 13	SG6: L Gar 5H 11	Arwood M. SG7: Bald 3D 12
Alington La. SG6: L Gar 2B 16	Arden Press Way Ind. Est.	Ascot Cres. SG1: Stev 6B 24
(not continuous)	SG6: L Gar 4H 11	Ascot Ind. Est. SG6: L Gar 4H 11
Alleyns Rd. SG1: Stev 2F 27	Arena Pde. SG6: L Gar 5F 11	Ashanger La. SG7: Clo 1D 18
Allison SG6: L Gar 6A 12	Argyle Way SG1: Stev 4E 27	Ashbourne Cl. SG6: L Gar 2D 16
Almonds La. SG1: Stev 6G 23	Argyle Way Trad. Est.	**ASHBROOK** **3G 21**
Alpine Cl. SG4: Hit 2E 21	SG1: Stev 4E 27	Ashbrook La. SG4: St Ipo 4F 21

Ashburnham Wlk. SG2: Stev . . . .2D 3_
Ashdown SG6: L Gar . . . . .2E 1_
Ashdown Rd. SG2: Stev . . . . . .4F 3_
Ash Dr. SG4: St Ipo . . . . .3E 2_
Ashleigh SG2: Stev . . . . .5B 2_
Ashton's La. SG7: Bald . . . . . . .5D 1_
Ashville Trad. Est. SG7: Bald . .2E 1_
Ashville Way SG7: Bald . . . . . .2E 1_
Ashwell SG1: Stev . . . . .5E 2_
(off Coreys Mill La_
Ashwell Cl. SG4: G'ley . . . . . . .3D 2_
Ashwell Comn. SG4: G'ley . . . .3D 2_
Ashwell Rd. SG7: Byg . . . . . . .1F 1_
SG7: New . . . . .1D _
Aspect One SG1: Stev . . . . . . .5D 2_
Aspen Cl. SG2: Stev . . . . .4F 3_
Aspen Pl. SG2: Stev . . . . .3D 3_
Aspens, The SG4: Hit . . . . .1E 2_
Asquith Ct. SG2: Stev . . . . . . .4G 3_
ASTON . . . .**1H 3_**
Aston Cl. SG1: Stev . . . . .5E 2_
(off Coreys Mill La_
ASTON END . . . .**4E 2_**
Aston End Rd. SG2: A'ton . . . . .6E 2_
Astonia Ho. SG7: Bald . . . . . . .4D 1_
(off High St_
Aston La. SG2: Stev . . . . .4H 3_

Aston Ri.—Chapel Row

Aston Ri. SG4: Hit 1F **21**
Astral Cl. SG16: H'low 6D **2**
Astwick Rd. SG5: Astw, Stot 1F **5**
Aubreys SG6: L Gar 3B **16**
Aubries SG2: Walk 6H **25**
Augustus Ga. SG2: Stev 1D **28**
Austen Paths SG2: Stev 3C **28**
Avenue, The SG1: Stev 1E **27**
SG4: Hit 6E **15**
SG5: Stot 3F **5**
Avenue One SG6: L Gar 4A **12**
Avocet SG6: L Gar 2E **11**
Avon Chase SG16: H'low 5E **3**
Avon Dr. SG1: Stev 4H **23**
Avon Rd. SG16: H'low 5E **3**
Aylward Dr. SG2: Stev 5B **28**
Ayr Cl. SG1: Stev 1C **28**

B

Babbage Rd. SG1: Stev 4C **26**
Back La. SG6: L Gar 5B **12**
SG7: Bald 4C **12**
Baddeley Cl. SG2: Stev 1F **31**
Bader Cl. SG1: Stev 6H **23**
Badger Cl. SG3: Kneb 5D **30**
Badgers Cl. SG1: Stev 5G **27**
Badminton Cl. SG2: Stev 4F **31**
Bakers M. SG4: Hit 4F **15**
Baker St. SG1: Stev 2E **27**
BALDOCK 3D **12**
Baldock By-Pass SG4: West 2G **17**
SG7: Bald 2G **17**
Baldock Ind. Est. SG7: Bald 4D **12**
Baldock La. SG6: Will 3D **16**
SG7: Bald 2E **17**
Baldock Rd. SG5: Stot 4G **5**
(not continuous)
SG6: L Gar 2B **16**
BALDOCK SERVICE AREA 3B **6**
Baldock Station (Rail) 2D **12**
Baliol Chambers *SG4: Hit 6D* ***14***
(off Hollow La.)
Baliol Rd. SG5: Hit 5D **14**
Balmoral Cl. SG2: Stev 4G **31**
Balmoral Rd. SG5: Hit 4C **14**
Bancroft SG5: Hit 6D **14**
Bancroft Ct. SG5: Hit 5C **14**
Bandley Ri. SG2: Stev 6C **28**
Barclay Cres. SG1: Stev 2G **27**
Barham Rd. SG2: Stev 4C **28**
Barleycroft SG2: Stev 6C **28**
Barley Ri. SG7: Bald 3F **13**
Barndell Cl. SG5: Stot 3F **5**
Barnwell SG2: Stev 6B **28**
Baron Ct. SG1: Stev 6D **22**
Barrington Rd. SG6: L Gar 1B **16**
(not continuous)
Barry Ct. *SG1: Stev 1D* ***26***
(off Huntingdon Rd.)
Basils Rd. SG1: Stev 2E **27**
Bassus Grn. Rd. SG2: Walk 6H **25**
Bates Ho. SG1: Stev 3G **27**
Bawdsey Cl. SG1: Stev 1D **26**
Bayworth SG6: L Gar 6H **11**
Beacons, The SG1: Stev 4B **24**
Beale Cl. SG2: Stev 3C **28**
Beane Av. SG2: Stev 3D **28**
Beane Wlk. SG2: Stev 3D **28**
Bearton Av. SG5: Hit 5C **14**
Bearton Cl. SG5: Hit 4C **14**
Bearton Ct. SG5: Hit 4C **14**
Bearton Grn. SG5: Hit 4B **14**
Bearton Rd. SG5: Hit 4B **14**
Beaumont Cl. SG5: Hit 5B **14**
Bedford Ho. SG1: Stev 3D **26**
Bedford Rd. SG5: Hol 1D **8**
SG6: L Gar 4D **10**
SG16: H'low, L Ston 4B **2**
Bedford St. SG5: Hit 6B **14**
BEDWELL 4H **27**
Bedwell Cres. SG1: Stev 4G **27**
Bedwell La. SG1: Stev 4G **27**
Bedwell Ri. SG1: Stev 4G **27**
Beech Dr. SG2: Stev 6B **28**
Beeches, The SG4: Hit 1E **21**
Beech Hill SG6: L Gar 4D **10**
Beech Ridge SG7: Bald 5D **12**
Beechwood Cl. SG5: Hit 3B **14**
SG7: Bald 6D **12**
Beecroft La. SG2: Walk 5H **25**
Belgrave M. SG2: Stev 3E **31**
Bell Acre SG6: L Gar 1D **16**
Bell Acre Gdns. SG6: L Gar 1D **16**
Bellamy Cl. SG3: Kneb 6D **30**
Bell Cl. SG3: Kneb 6E **31**
SG4: Hit 1F **21**
Bell La. SG1: Stev 2E **27**
Bell Row SG7: Bald 3C **12**
Benbroke Pl. SG1: West 3B **24**
Benchley Hill SG4: Hit 5G **15**
Benington Rd. SG2: A'ton 1H **31**
SG2: Walk 2G **29**
Bennett Ct. SG6: L Gar 6G **11**
(Holmdale)
SG6: L Gar 5F **11**
(Station Rd.)
Benslow La. SG4: Hit 6E **15**
Benslow Pl. SG4: Hit 6E **15**
Benslow Ri. SG4: Hit 6E **15**
Benstede SG2: Stev 3G **31**
Berkeley SG6: L Gar 1C **16**
Berkeley Cl. SG2: Stev 3E **31**
SG5: Hit 5B **14**
Bernhardt Cres. SG2: Stev 3C **28**
Bertram Ho. SG1: Stev 3G **27**
Berwick Cl. SG1: Stev 1C **26**
Bessemer Cl. SG5: Hit 3C **14**
Bessemer Dr. SG1: Stev 5D **26**
Beverley Rd. SG1: Stev 5B **24**
Bidwell Cl. SG6: L Gar 6H **11**
Biggin, The *SG5: Hit 1D* ***20***
(off Biggin La.)
Biggin La. SG5: Hit 1D **20**
Bilton Rd. SG4: Hit 3D **14**
Bingen Rd. SG5: Hit 4A **14**
Birches, The SG6: L Gar 3E **11**
Birch Gro. SG16: L Ston 6C **2**
Birds Hill SG6: L Gar 5G **11**
Bittern Cl. SG2: Stev 1H **31**
Bittern Way SG6: L Gar 2E **11**
Blackberry Mead SG2: Stev 6D **28**
Blackdown Cl. SG1: Stev 4B **24**
Blackhorse Cl. SG4: Hit 2E **21**
Blackhorse La. SG4: Hit 3D **20**
Blackhorse Rd. SG6: L Gar 3A **12**
Blackmore SG6: L Gar 2D **16**
Blacksmiths Cl. SG5: Stot 2F **5**
Bladon Cl. SG4: L Wym 4B **22**
Blair Cl. SG2: Stev 2D **30**
Blakemore End Rd.
SG4: L Wym 5H **21**
Blakeney Ho. SG1: Stev 2C **26**
Blakeney Rd. SG1: Stev 2C **26**
Blenheim Way SG2: Stev 4G **31**
Bloomfield Ho. SG1: Stev 3G **27**
Bluebell Dr. SG16: L Ston 6C **2**
Blyth Cl. SG1: Stev 2C **26**
Bockings SG2: Walk 6H **25**
Bodnor Ga. SG7: Bald 3D **12**
Bondor Ind. Cen. SG7: Bald 4D **12**
Borton Av. SG16: H'low 5D **2**
Boscombe Ct. SG6: L Gar 5H **11**
Boswell Dr. SG5: Ick 1C **14**
Boswell Gdns. SG1: Stev 6F **23**
Botany Bay La. SG1: Stev 4A **24**
Botany Lodge SG1: Stev 4B **24**
Boulton Rd. SG1: Stev 5C **24**
Bournemouth Rd. SG1: Stev 1D **26**
Bowcock Wlk. SG1: Stev 6G **27**
Bowershott SG6: L Gar 1C **16**
Bowes Lyon Cen. 4G **27**
Bowling Grn. SG1: Stev 1E **27**
Bowmans Av. SG4: Hit 6F **15**
Bowman Trad. Est.
SG1: Stev 4D **26**
Bowyer's Cl. SG5: Hit 4B **14**
Boxberry Cl. SG1: Stev 3G **27**
Boxfield Grn. SG2: Stev 1D **28**
Bradleys Cnr. SG4: Hit 4G **15**
Bradman Way SG1: Stev 6A **24**
Bradshaw Ct. SG2: Stev 6B **28**
Braemar Cl. SG2: Stev 4F **31**
Bragbury Cl. SG2: Stev 4H **31**
BRAGBURY END 4H **31**
Bragbury La. SG2: Stev 5H **31**
SG3: Dat 5H **31**
Braham Ct. *SG5: Hit 6C* ***14***
(off Nun's Cl.)
Brambles, The SG1: Stev 5F **23**
Bramfield SG4: Hit 1F **21**
Bramley Cl. SG7: Bald 2D **12**
Brampton Pk. Rd. SG5: Hit 4C **14**
Bramshott Cl. SG4: Hit 3D **20**
Brandles Rd. SG6: L Gar 2C **16**
Brand St. SG5: Hit 6C **14**
Braunds All. SG5: Hit 6C **14**
Bray Dr. SG1: Stev 4A **24**
Brayes Mnr. SG5: Stot 3F **5**
Breakspear SG2: Stev 6C **28**
Brent Ct. SG1: Stev 4G **27**
Brewery La. SG7: Bald 2C **12**
Briardale SG1: Stev 5G **27**
Briar Patch La. SG6: L Gar 2H **15**
Brick Kiln La.
SG4: C'ton, Hit 2B **20**
Brick Kiln Rd. SG1: Stev 3E **27**
Bridge Rd. SG1: Stev 2D **26**
SG6: L Gar 5F **11**
Bridge Rd. W. SG1: Stev 3D **26**
Bridge St. SG5: Hit 1C **20**
Brighton Way SG1: Stev 1C **26**
British Schools Mus. 1D **20**
Brittains Ri. SG16: L Ston 1A **8**
Brittain Way SG2: Stev 5B **28**
Brixham Cl. SG1: Stev 2D **26**
Broadcroft SG6: L Gar 3B **16**
Broadhall Way SG1: Stev 1B **30**
SG2: Stev 2G **31**
Broadmead SG4: Hit 2E **21**
Broadmeadow Ride
SG4: St Ipo 3E **21**
Broad Oak Way SG2: Stev 1D **30**
Broadview SG1: Stev 3G **27**
BROADWATER 3E **31**
Broadwater SG2: Stev 2F **31**
Broadwater Av. SG6: L Gar 6E **11**
Broadwater Cres. SG2: Stev 1D **30**
Broadwater Dale SG6: L Gar 6E **11**
Broadwater La.
SG2: A'ton, Stev 2G **31**
Broadway SG6: L Gar 1A **16**
Brockwell Shott SG2: Walk 6H **25**
Bronte Av. SG5: L Gar 1C **10**
Bronte Paths SG2: Stev 3C **28**
Brook Cl. SG16: H'low 2A **2**
Brook Dr. SG2: Stev 3F **31**
BROOK END 4E **5**
Brookfield SG2: A'ton 6E **29**
Brookfield La.
SG2: A'ton, Ast E 5F **29**
Brookhill SG2: Stev 3D **30**
Brookside SG6: L Gar 6F **11**
Brook St. SG5: Stot 3E **5**
Brookvale SG16: U Sto 6A **2**
Brook Vw. SG4: Hit 1G **21**
Broom Gro. SG3: Kneb 6D **30**
Broom Wlk. SG1: Stev 4G **27**
Broughton Hill SG6: L Gar 5G **11**
Browning Dr. SG4: Hit 5F **15**
Broxdell SG1: Stev 3G **27**
Brunel Rd. SG2: Stev 2A **28**
Brunel Wlk. SG5: L Gar 1C **10**
Bucklersbury SG5: Hit 1C **20**
Buckthorn Av. SG1: Stev 5G **27**
Bude Cres. SG1: Stev 2C **26**
Bulwer Link SG1: Stev 6G **27**
Bunyan Cl. SG5: Pirt 6A **8**
Bunyan Rd. SG5: Hit 5C **14**
Burford Way SG5: Hit 3A **14**
Burgess Way SG16: H'low 1A **2**
Burghley Cl. SG2: Stev 3E **31**
Burley SG6: L Gar 2F **11**
Burnell Ri. SG6: L Gar 6D **10**
Burnell Wlk. SG6: L Gar 6E **11**
Burnett Av. SG16: H'low 5D **2**
Burns Cl. SG2: Stev 1C **28**
SG4: Hit 5F **15**
Burnthouse La. SG7: Clo 2F **19**
Bursland SG6: L Gar 5D **10**
Burwell Rd. SG2: Stev 5B **28**
Burydale SG2: Stev 2F **31**
Bury Mead SG15: Arl 2A **4**
Burymead SG1: Stev 6E **23**
Bury Mead Rd. SG5: Hit 3D **14**
Bush Spring SG7: Bald 2E **13**
Business & Technology Cen.
SG1: Stev 4D **26**
Business Cen. E. SG6: L Gar 5A **12**
Business Cen. W.
SG6: L Gar 5A **12**
Butchers La. SG4: Hit 2D **20**
Butlers Yd. SG7: Bald 2C **12**
Butterfield Ct. SG7: Bald 3C **12**
Butts Grn. SG4: West 4C **18**
BYGRAVE 4G **7**
Bygrave *SG1: Stev 5E* ***23***
(off Coreys Mill La.)
Bygrave Rd. SG7: Bald 2D **12**
Byrd Wlk. SG7: Bald 4D **12**
Byron Cl. SG2: Stev 2C **28**
SG4: Hit 5F **15**

C

Cabot Cl. SG2: Stev 2A **28**
Cade Cl. SG6: L Gar 2A **12**
CADWELL 6H **9**
Cadwell Ct. SG4: Hit 3E **15**
Cadwell Grn. SG4: Hit 3E **15**
Cadwell La. SG4: Hit 3D **14**
Caernarvon Cl. SG2: Stev 4F **31**
Caister Cl. SG1: Stev 6C **22**
Caldecote Rd. SG7: New 1B **6**
Calder Way SG1: Stev 4A **24**
California SG7: Bald 2D **12**
Cambridge Rd. SG4: Hit 5F **15**
Cam Cen. SG4: Hit 2E **15**
Cameron Cl. SG2: Stev 2B **28**
Campbell Cl. SG4: Hit 5F **15**
Campers Av. SG6: L Gar 6E **11**
Campers Rd. SG6: L Gar 6D **10**
Campers Wlk. SG6: L Gar 6E **11**
Campfield Way SG6: L Gar 6D **10**
Campion Ct. SG1: Stev 1E **27**
Campkin Mead SG2: Stev 6D **28**
Campshill La. SG2: Stev 3A **28**
Campus Five SG6: L Gar 4A **12**
Cam Sq. SG4: Hit 2E **15**
Cannix Cl. SG2: Stev 1E **31**
Cannon Ho. *SG4: Hit 1D* ***20***
(off Queen St.)
Cannons Health Club
Letchworth Garden City
3B **16**
Canterbury Way SG1: Stev 6G **23**
Cardiff Cl. SG2: Stev 4F **31**
Carling Pl. SG5: Hit 3B **14**
Carters Cl. SG2: Stev 5D **28**
SG15: Arl 2A **4**
Carters Wlk. SG15: Arl 2A **4**
Carters Way SG15: Arl 2A **4**
Cartwright Rd. SG1: Stev 5C **24**
Cashio La. SG6: L Gar 2G **11**
Caslon Way SG6: L Gar 2F **11**
Castings Ho. SG6: L Gar 4G **11**
Castle Ct. SG5: Hit 4B **14**
Castles Cl. SG5: Stot 1F **5**
Cavalier *SG1: Stev 6D* ***22***
(off Ingleside Dr.)
SG1: Stev 5A ***24***
(off Pilgrims Way)
Cavell Wlk. SG2: Stev 4C **28**
(not continuous)
SG5: L Gar 1D **10**
Cavendish Rd. SG1: Stev 4C **26**
Caxton Ga. SG1: Stev 5D **26**
Caxton Pl. SG1: Stev 5D **26**
Caxton Way SG1: Stev 5D **26**
Cedar Av. SG5: Ick 1C **14**
Cemetery Rd. SG4: Hit 1D **20**
Central App. SG6: L Gar 5F **11**
Central Av. SG16: H'low 6D **2**
Centre 24 SG6: L Gar 3B **12**
Chace, The SG2: Stev 2D **30**
Chadwell Rd. SG1: Stev 5D **26**
Chagny Cl. SG6: L Gar 5E **11**
Chalkdell Path SG5: Hit 5B **14**
Chalkdown SG2: Stev 2D **28**
Chalk Fld. SG6: L Gar 2E **17**
Chalk Hills SG7: Bald 6D **12**
Chambers Ga. SG1: Stev 2F **27**
Chambers La. SG5: Ick 1C **14**
Chancellors SG15: Arl 2B **4**
Chancellors Rd. SG1: Stev 6E **23**
Chantry La. SG4: L Wym 5B **22**
Chaomans SG6: L Gar 2B **16**
Chapel Dr. SG15: Arl 5A **4**
Chapel Pl. SG5: Stot 4F **5**
Chapel Rd. SG17: Mepp 3A **2**
Chapel Row *SG5: Hit 5D* ***14***
(off Whinbush Rd.)

Chapel Way—Firs Cl.

Chapel Way SG16: H'low 2A **2**
Chapman Rd. SG1: Stev 6D **22**
Chapmans, The SG5: Hit 1C **20**
CHARLTON 2B **20**
Charlton Rd.
SG4: C'ton, Pres 5A **20**
SG5: C'ton, Hit 3A **20**
Chase, The SG15: Arl 3A **4**
Chase Cl. SG15: Arl 1A **4**
Chase Hill Rd. SG15: Arl 3A **4**
Chasten Hill SG6: L Gar 4D **10**
Chatsworth Ct. SG2: Stev 2D **30**
Chatterton SG6: L Gar 6H **11**
Chaucer Way SG4: Hit 5G **15**
Chauncy Gdns. SG7: Bald 2F **13**
Chauncy Ho. SG1: Stev 3G **27**
Chauncy Rd. SG1: Stev 3G **27**
CHELLS 3C **28**
Chells Ent. Village
SG2: Stev 3C **28**
Chells La. SG2: Stev 2C **28**
(not continuous)
CHELLS MANOR 1D **28**
Chells Way SG2: Stev 2A **28**
Chennells Cl. SG4: Hit 3F **15**
Chepstow Cl. SG1: Stev 1B **28**
Chequers Bri. Rd.
SG1: Stev 3E **27**
Chequers Cl. SG5: Stot 3G **5**
Cherry Cl. SG3: Kneb 6G **31**
Cherry Tree Cl. SG15: Arl 5A **4**
Cherry Tree Ri. SG2: Walk 1H **29**
Cherry Trees SG16: L Ston 6D **2**
Cherry Trees Dr. SG2: Stev 2B **28**
Chertsey Ri. SG2: Stev 5C **28**
Cherwell Dr. SG1: Stev 4A **24**
Chester Rd. SG1: Stev 6A **24**
Chestnut Av. SG16: H'low 6D **2**
Chestnut Ct. SG5: Hit 5B **14**
Chestnut Farm SG16: H'low 2A **2**
Chestnut Wlk. SG1: Stev 6F **23**
SG4: St Ipo 3E **21**
Cheviot Way SG1: West 3A **24**
Childwock Way SG6: L Gar 3E **11**
Chiltern Pl. SG16: H'low 2A **2**
Chiltern Rd. SG4: Hit 6E **15**
SG7: Bald 5D **12**
Chilterns, The SG1: Stev 4B **24**
SG4: Hit 1E **21**
Chiltern Vw. SG6: L Gar 6D **10**
Chilvers Bank SG7: Bald 4C **12**
Cholwell Rd. SG2: Stev 6C **28**
Chouler Gdns. SG1: Stev 5E **23**
Christie Rd. SG2: Stev 4C **28**
CHURCH END
SG4 . . . . .4D **18**
SG15 . . . . .2A **4**
Church End SG2: Walk 5H **25**
SG15: Arl 1A **4**
Churchgate SG5: Hit 1C **20**
Church Grn. SG4: Gt Wym 1A **22**
Church La. SG1: Stev 2E **27**
SG4: G'ley 3E **23**
SG4: West 5D **18**
SG6: Nort 2A **12**
SG15: Arl 1A **4**
Church Path SG4: L Wym 4B **22**
SG5: Ick 1C **14**
Church Rd. SG5: Stot 3F **5**
SG16: H'low 1A **2**
Church St. SG7: Bald 2C **12**
Churchyard SG5: Hit 6C **14**
Churchyard Wlk. SG5: Hit 6C **14**
Cineworld
Stevenage 5E **27**
Clare Cres. SG7: Bald 5C **12**
Clare Gdns. SG5: Hit 6D **14**
Claybush Rd. SG7: Ashw 1H **7**
Claymore Dr. SG5: Ick 6H **9**
Claymores SG1: Stev 3G **27**
Cleveland Way SG1: Stev 4C **24**
SG1: West 4C **24**
Cleviscroft SG1: Stev 5G **27**
Clifton Rd. SG16: H'low 2A **2**
Cloister Lawn SG6: L Gar 1B **16**
Cloisters Rd. SG6: L Gar 1B **16**
Close, The SG1: Stev 6E **23**
SG7: Bald 4C **12**
CLOTHALL 1D **18**
Clothall Rd. SG7: Bald 3D **12**
Clovelly Way SG1: Stev 1C **26**
Cluny Way SG15: Arl 4A **4**
Coach Dr. SG4: Hit 2D **20**
Coach Ho. Cloisters
SG7: Bald 3C **12**
Coachman's La.
SG7: Bald 3B **12**
Coach Rd. SG16: H'low 2A **2**
Cockerell Cl. SG1: Stev 3D **26**
Codicote Ho. *SG1: Stev 6E* ***23***
(off Coreys Mill La.)
Coleridge Cl. SG4: Hit 5F **15**
Colestrete SG1: Stev 5H **27**
Colestrete Cl. SG1: Stev 4A **28**
College Rd. SG5: Hit 5D **14**
Collenswood Rd. SG2: Stev . . .5B **28**
Collison Cl. SG4: Hit 3G **15**
Colonnade, The *SG6: L Gar 5F* ***11***
(off Eastcheap)
Colts Cnr. SG2: Stev 5B **28**
Columbus Cl. SG2: Stev 2A **28**
Colwyn Cl. SG1: Stev 2D **26**
Commerce Way SG6: L Gar 5F **11**
Common Ri. SG4: Hit 4E **15**
Common Rd. SG5: Stot 1F **5**
Common Vw. SG6: L Gar 3G **11**
Common Vw. Sq.
SG6: L Gar 3G **11**
Conifer Cl. SG2: Stev 2D **28**
Conifer Wlk. SG2: Stev 2C **28**
Connelly La. *SG5: L Gar 1D* ***10***
(off Bronte Av.)
Conquest Cl. SG4: Hit 2D **20**
Constantine Cl. SG1: Stev 6H **23**
Constantine Pl. SG7: Bald 2F **13**
Convent Cl. SG5: Hit 5D **14**
Cook Rd. SG2: Stev 2B **28**
Cooks Way SG4: Hit 4E **15**
Cooper Cl. SG16: L Ston 1A **8**
Coopers All. SG5: Hit 6C **14**
Coopers Cl. SG2: Stev 5D **28**
Coopers Fld. SG6: L Gar 4D **10**
Coppens, The SG5: Stot 4G **5**
Copperfield Cl. SG5: L Gar 1C **10**
Coppice Mead SG5: Stot 4E **5**
Coreys Mill La. SG1: Stev 6D **22**
Corner Cl. SG6: L Gar 5E **11**
Cornfields SG2: Stev 2C **28**
Corton Cl. SG1: Stev 1D **26**
Cotney Cft. SG2: Stev 6D **28**
Cotswold Dr. SG1: West 3A **24**
Cotter Ho. SG1: Stev 4A **24**
Cotton Brown Pk.
SG6: L Gar 4A **12**
Coventry Cl. SG1: Stev 6A **24**
Cowslip Hill SG6: L Gar 4E **11**
Cox's Way SG15: Arl 3A **4**
Crabbes Cl. SG5: Hit 6C **14**
Crabtree Dell SG6: L Gar 2E **17**
Crabtree La. SG7: Bald 5C **12**
Crabtree Rd. SG3: Kneb 6G **31**
Cragside SG2: Stev 4G **31**
Cranborne *SG1: Stev 6D* ***22***
(off Ingleside Dr.)
Cranborne Av. SG5: Hit 1B **20**
Creamery Ct. SG6: L Gar 2E **17**
Crescent, The SG4: St Ipo 4E **21**
SG5: Hit 4B **14**
SG6: L Gar 6G **11**
SG16: H'low 5E **3**
Cricketer's Rd. SG15: Arl 5A **4**
Crispin Ter. SG5: Hit 5B **14**
Croft Ct. SG5: Hit 6C **14**
Croft La. SG6: L Gar 2G **11**
Crofts, The SG5: Stot 3F **5**
Cromdale Wlk. SG1: West 3B **24**
Crompton Rd. SG1: Stev 3C **26**
Cromwell Grn. SG6: L Gar 3H **11**
Cromwell Rd. SG2: Stev 4C **28**
SG6: L Gar 3H **11**
Cromwell Way SG5: Pirt 6A **8**
Crossgates SG1: Stev 4G **27**
Crossleys SG6: L Gar 1F **11**
Cross St. SG6: L Gar 4F **11**
Crossways Cl. SG16: H'low 1F **3**
Crow End SG4: G'ley 3F **23**
Crow Furlong SG5: Hit 1B **20**
Crown Lodge SG15: Arl 5A **4**
Cubitt Cl. SG4: Hit 6G **15**
Culrose Ct. SG2: Stev 3D **30**
Curlew Cl. SG6: L Gar 2E **11**
Cuttys La. SG1: Stev 4G **27**

D

Dacre Rd. SG5: Hit 5E **15**
Dagnalls SG6: L Gar 3B **16**
Dairy, The SG16: H'low 2A **2**
Daisy Ct. SG6: L Gar 3G **11**
Dale, The SG6: L Gar 6E **11**
Dale Cl. SG4: Hit 3D **20**
Daltry Cl. SG1: Stev 5E **23**
Daltry Rd. SG1: Stev 5E **23**
(not continuous)
Damask Cl. SG4: West 5B **18**
DAMASK GREEN 5B **18**
Damask Grn. Rd. SG4: West . . .5B **18**
Dancote SG3: Kneb 6D **30**
Dane Cl. SG5: Stot 1F **5**
Dane End Ho. *SG1: Stev 6E* ***23***
(off Coreys Mill La.)
Dane End La. SG4: West 3E **25**
Danescroft SG6: L Gar 2F **11**
Danesgate SG1: Stev 5F **27**
Daneshill Ho. *SG1: Stev 4F* ***27***
(off Danestrete)
Danestrete SG1: Stev 4F **27**
Darwin Rd. SG2: Stev 3B **28**
David Evans Ct. SG6: L Gar . . .4D **10**
David Lloyd Leisure
Stevenage 5E **27**
Davidson Ct. *SG6: L Gar 5H* ***11***
(off Bidwell Cl.)
Davis Cres. SG5: Pirt 6A **8**
Davis Row SG15: Arl 5A **4**
Dawlish Cl. SG2: Stev 4G **31**
Dawson Cl. SG16: H'low 4E **3**
Deacons Way SG5: Hit 4B **14**
Deanscroft SG3: Kneb 6D **30**
Deard's End La. SG3: Kneb 5D **30**
Deards Wood SG3: Kneb 6D **30**
Deeping Cl. SG3: Kneb 6G **31**
Dell, The SG1: Stev 4G **27**
SG7: Bald 5C **12**
Denby SG6: L Gar 1D **16**
Dene La. SG2: A'ton 1H **31**
Denton Rd. SG1: Stev 5G **27**
Dents Cl. SG6: L Gar 2E **17**
Derby Way SG1: Stev 1B **28**
Derwent Rd. SG16: H'low 5D **2**
Desborough Rd. SG4: Hit 5G **15**
Devonshire Cl. SG2: Stev 3E **31**
Dewpond Cl. SG1: Stev 1E **27**
Diamond Ind. Cen.
SG6: L Gar 4A **12**
Dickens Blvd. SG5: L Gar 1C **10**
Ditchmore La. SG1: Stev 3F **27**
Doncaster Cl. SG1: Stev 1C **28**
Dorchester Ho. *SG6: L Gar 5F* ***11***
(off Station Rd.)
Douglas Dr. SG1: Stev 1A **28**
Dovedale SG2: Stev 5B **28**
Dove Ho. Dr. SG16: H'low 1F **3**
Dovehouse La. SG2: Walk 5G **25**
Dove Rd. SG1: Stev 4H **23**
Dower Ct. *SG4: Hit 2D* ***20***
(off London Rd.)
Downlands SG2: Stev 2D **28**
SG7: Bald 2E **13**
Drakes Dr. SG2: Stev 2B **28**
Drapers Way SG1: Stev 2E **27**
Dryden Cres. SG2: Stev 1B **28**
Dugdale Ct. SG5: Hit 4A **14**
Duke's La. SG5: Hit 5D **14**
Duncots Cl. SG5: Ick 2C **14**
Dunham's La. SG6: L Gar 4H **11**
Dunkerley Ct. SG6: L Gar 4G **11**
Dunlin SG6: L Gar 2E **11**
Dunn Cl. SG1: Stev 6G **27**
Dunwich Farm SG1: Stev 3C **26**
Durham Rd. SG1: Stev 6A **24**
Dyes La. SG1: Stev 6B **26**
SG4: Lang 5A **26**
Dymoke M. SG1: Stev 1E **27**

E

Eagle Ct. SG7: Bald 2C **12**
Earlsmead SG6: L Gar 2B **16**
Earnshaw Av. SG5: L Gar 1B **10**
Eastbourne Av. SG1: Stev 3C **26**
Eastcheap SG6: L Gar 5F **11**
East Cl. SG1: Stev 4H **27**
SG4: Hit 4F **15**
Eastern Av. SG16: H'low 6E **3**
Eastern Way SG6: L Gar 3G **11**
Eastgate SG1: Stev 5F **27**
Easthall Ho. *SG1: Stev 5E* ***23***
(off Coreys Mill La.)
Eastholm SG6: L Gar 3G **11**
Eastholm Grn. SG6: L Gar 3G **11**
Eastman Way SG1: Stev 5C **24**
East Reach SG2: Stev 1E **31**
East Vw. SG4: St Ipo 5G **21**
Edgeworth Cl. SG2: Stev 2G **31**
Edison Rd. SG2: Stev 3B **28**
Edmonds Dr. SG2: Stev 5D **28**
Edwards Ho. SG1: Stev 3G **27**
Eisenberg Cl. SG7: Bald 2F **13**
Elbow La. SG2: Stev 3F **31**
Eldefield SG6: L Gar 4C **10**
Elderberry Dr. SG4: St Ipo 3E **21**
Elderflower Ho. *SG5: Hit 6D* ***14***
(off Whinbush Rd.)
Elder Way SG1: Stev 6F **27**
Elgin Ho. SG4: Hit 1E **21**
Eliot Rd. SG2: Stev 3C **28**
Elizabeth Ct. SG16: H'low 2A **2**
Ellice SG6: L Gar 1D **16**
Ellis Av. SG1: Stev 1G **27**
Elm Cl. SG16: H'low 2A **2**
Elm Pk. SG7: Bald 3D **12**
Elms Cl. SG4: L Wym 4A **22**
Elmside Wlk. SG5: Hit 5C **14**
Elm Wlk. SG2: Stev 6B **28**
Elmwood Av. SG7: Bald 4D **12**
Elmwood Ct. SG7: Bald 3D **12**
Ely Cl. SG1: Stev 5B **24**
Emperors Ga. SG2: Stev 1D **28**
Endeavour Cl. SG16: L Ston 6B **2**
Enjakes Cl. SG2: Stev 4F **31**
Ennismore Cl. SG6: L Gar 2D **16**
Epsom Cl. SG1: Stev 1B **28**
ERNEST GARDINER DAY HOSPITAL
. . . . .6H **11**
Essex Ho. SG1: Stev 3D **26**
Essex Rd. SG1: Stev 1D **26**
Everest Cl. SG15: Arl 4B **4**
Exchange, The SG4: Hit 6D **14**
Exchange Rd. SG1: Stev 4H **27**
Exchange Yd. SG5: Hit 6C **14**
Exeter Cl. SG1: Stev 5B **24**
Eynsford Ct. SG4: Hit 1D **20**

F

Fairfield Cres. SG1: West 3B **24**
Fairfield Hall SG5: Stot 6C **4**
Fairfield Way SG1: Stev 4C **24**
SG4: Hit 5H **15**
Fairlands Valley Sailing Club
. . . . .4A **28**
Fairlands Way SG1: Stev 4E **27**
Fairview Rd. SG1: Stev 1D **26**
Fakeswell La. SG16: L Ston 1A **8**
Falcon Cl. SG2: Stev 1H **31**
Fallowfield SG2: Stev 6C **28**
Faraday Gdns. SG5: L Gar 1C **10**
Faraday Rd. SG2: Stev 3B **28**
Farm Cl. SG1: Stev 5G **27**
SG6: L Gar 2G **11**
Farriers Cl. SG7: Bald 2C **12**
Farthing Dr. SG6: L Gar 2E **17**
Fawcett Rd. SG2: Stev 1B **2**
Fearnhill Sports Cen. 6C **1**
Featherston Rd. SG2: Stev 6C **2**
Fellowes Way SG2: Stev 1D **3**
Fells Cl. SG5: Hit 5D **14**
Fen End SG5: Stot 1F
Ferrier Rd. SG2: Stev 3C **2**
Fieldfare SG2: Stev 6D **2**
SG6: L Gar 2E **1**
Fieldgate Ho. SG1: Stev 4H **2**
Field La. SG6: L Gar 1B **1**
Fifth Av. SG6: L Gar 5A **1**
Filey Cl. SG1: Stev 2C **2**
Finbracks SG1: West 3A **2**
Finches, The SG4: Hit 6E **1**
Finches End SG2: Walk 1H **2**
Fir Cl. SG2: Stev 2D **3**
Firecrest SG6: L Gar 2E **1**
Firs Cl. SG5: Hit 5B **1**

34 A-Z Stevenage

First Garden City Heritage Mus.
..........6G 11
FISHER'S GREEN 2C 26
Fishers Grn. SG1: Stev 6C 22
(not continuous)
Fishers Grn. Cen. SG1: Stev ..1D 26
Fishersgreen La. SG1: Stev ..6D 22
Fisher's Grn. Rd. SG1: Stev ..1D 26
Fishponds SG5: Hit 5C 14
Fitness First
Stevenage 6G 27
Fleetwood SG6: L Gar 1D 16
Fleetwood Cres. SG1: Stev ..1D 26
Fleming Dr. SG5: L Gar 1D 10
Flight Path SG16: H'low 6D 2
Flinders Cl. SG2: Stev 4C 28
Flint Rd. SG4: Gar 3A 12
Florence St. SG5: Hit 5D 14
Folly Cl. SG5: Hit 2E 21
Folly Path SG4: Hit 1D 20
Football Cl. SG7: Bald 2C 12
Fordham Courtyard SG5: Stot ...4E 5
Fore St. SG4: West 4B 18
Forest Row SG2: Stev 2D 30
Forge Cl. SG5: Hit 5D 14
Forge End SG4: West 4C 18
Fortuna SG1: Stev 1C 28
Forum, The SG1: Stev 4F 27
Fosman Cl. SG5: Hit 5B 14
Foster Cl. SG1: Stev 6F 23
Foster Dr. SG4: Hit 2E 21
Four Acres SG1: Stev 2F 27
Fouracres SG6: L Gar 2C 16
Fourth Av. SG6: L Gar 4A 12
Fovant SG1: Stev 6D 22
Foxfield SG2: Stev 6C 28
Fox Rd. SG1: Stev 4G 27
Foyle Cl. SG4: Hit 4C 24
Francis Cl. SG4: Hit 2E 21
SG5: Stot 3E 5
Franklin Gdns. SG4: Hit 4F 15
Franklin's Rd. SG1: Stev 1E 27
Franks Cl. SG16: H'low 5D 2
Frank Young Cl. SG5: Hit 4B 14
Fraser Cnr. SG2: Stev 1B 28
Fred Millard Cl. SG1: Stev ..4G 27
Freeman's Cl. SG5: Hit 4B 14
Freewaters Cl. SG5: Ick 1C 14
French Lodge SG5: Hit 5D 14
Frensham Dr. SG4: Hit 3G 15
Fresson Rd. SG1: Stev 1F 27
Friars Rd. SG4: West 4B 18
Friday Furlong SG5: Hit 5A 14
Friends Grn. SG4: West 1B 24
Frobisher Dr. SG2: Stev 2B 28
Froghall La. SG2: Walk 6G 25
Frogmore Ho. SG1: Stev 5E 23
(off Coreys Mill La.)
Fry Rd. SG2: Stev 4C 28
Fullers Ct. SG6: L Gar 4E 11
Fulton Cl. SG1: Stev 4E 27
Furlay Cl. SG6: L Gar 4D 10
Furmston Ct. SG6: L Gar 4G 11
Furzedown SG2: Stev 5B 28
Fyfies Cl. SG5: Hit 5D 14

G

Gainsford Cres. SG4: Hit 3G 15
Gallery, The SG6: L Gar 5F 11
(off Openshaw Way)
Galleywood SG5: Ick 1B 14
Gaping La. SG5: Hit 6B 14
Gardeners La. SG16: H'low ...1A 2
GARDEN HOUSE HOSPICE ...6H 11
Garden Row SG5: Hit 5D 14
Gardens, The SG5: Stot 3E 5
SG6: L Gar 1B 16
SG7: Bald 3C 12
SG16: H'low 1F 3
Garden Wlk. SG1: Stev 4G 27
Garrison Ct. SG4: Hit 6D 14
Garth Rd. SG6: L Gar 2A 16
Gates Way SG1: Stev 3E 27
Gaunts Way SG6: L Gar 1F 11
Gaylor Way SG1: Stev 1F 27
Gentle Ct. SG7: Bald 3C 12
George Leighton Ct.
SG2: Stev 4B 28
Georgina Ct. SG15: Arl 6A 4

Gernon Rd. SG6: L Gar 6F 11
Gernon Wlk. SG6: L Gar 6F 11
(not continuous)
Gibbons Way SG3: Kneb 6D 30
Gibson Cl. SG4: Hit 6F 15
Gillison Cl. SG6: L Gar 6H 11
Gipsy La. SG3: Kneb 6C 30
Girdle Rd. SG4: Hit 3E 15
Girons Cl. SG4: Hit 1F 21
Glade, The SG6: L Gar 2D 16
SG7: Bald 4C 12
Gladstone Cl. SG2: Stev 3E 31
Gladstone Dr. SG5: Stot 1D 10
Glebe, The SG2: Stev 3C 28
Glebe Av. SG15: Arl 2A 4
Glebe Cl. SG4: Hit 5G 21
Glebe Meadows Nature Reserve
..........2H 3
Glebe Rd. SG6: L Gar 4G 11
Glebe Rd. Ind. Est.
SG6: L Gar 4G 11
Glebe Vw. SG2: Walk 5H 25
(not continuous)
Glenwood Cl. SG2: Stev 1G 31
Glossop Way SG15: Arl 2B 4
Gloucester Cl. SG1: Stev 5G 23
Glover Cen., The SG5: Hit ...4D 14
Glovers Ct. SG5: Hit 4D 14
Glynde, The SG2: Stev 3F 31
Goddard End SG2: Stev 2G 31
Godfrey Cl. SG2: Stev 6B 28
Golden Willows Site
SG5: Ick 5G 9
Goldon SG2: Stev 1E 17
Gonville Cres. SG2: Stev 1G 31
Gordian Way SG2: Stev 6C 24
Gordon Ct. SG3: Kneb 6E 31
Gordon Craig Theatre, The ...4F 27
(off Lytton Way)
Gorleston Cl. SG1: Stev 6C 22
Gorst Cl. SG6: L Gar 6E 11
GOSMORE 4D 20
Gosmore SG1: Stev 5E 23
(off Coreys Mill La.)
Gosmore Ley Cl. SG4: Gos ...4D 20
Gosmore Rd. SG4: Hit 2D 20
Gothic Way SG15: Arl 4A 4
Grace Way SG1: Stev 6G 23
Grammar School Wlk.
SG5: Hit 6C 14
Grampian Pl. SG1: West 4B 24
Granary, The SG15: Arl 4A 4
Granby Rd. SG1: Stev 5E 23
Grange, The SG1: Stev 1E 27
Grange Cl. SG4: Hit 3E 21
Grange Ct. SG6: L Gar 2G 11
Grange Dr. SG5: Stot 4F 5
Grange Rd. SG6: L Gar 3F 11
Granville Rd. SG4: Hit 4G 15
Grasmere SG1: Stev 4C 24
Grass Mdws. SG2: Stev 2D 28
GRAVELEY 3E 23
Graveley Cl. SG1: Stev 5E 23
(off Coreys Mill La.)
Graveley La.
SG4: G'ley, Gt Wym 2B 22
Graveley Rd. SG1: Stev 4D 22
SG4: Gt Wym 1A 22
Gray's La. SG5: Hit 6B 14
GREAT ASHBY 4C 24
Gt. Ashby Way SG1: Stev ...5G 23
Great Gables SG1: West 3A 24
Great Nth. Rd. SG1: Stev ...5E 23
SG4: G'ley 2E 23
SG7: Bald 6C 6
SG4: Cald, Hinx 1H 5
GREAT WYMONDLEY 1A 22
Green, The SG3: Old K 6A 30
SG4: West 4B 18
SG5: Stot 2F 5
SG7: New 2C 6
Green Acres SG2: Stev 2G 31
Green Cl. SG2: Stev 1E 31
GREEN END 3C 18
Greenfield Av. SG5: Ick 1B 14
Greenfield Cl. SG5: Ick 1C 14
Greenfield Rd. SG1: Stev 2G 27
Green La. SG4: Hit 4F 15
SG6: L Gar 2H 11
Green Lane 3 SG6: L Gar ...4A 12
Green La. Ct. SG4: Hit 4F 15

Greenside Dr. SG5: Hit 5B 14
Green St. SG1: Stev 2E 27
Greenway SG2: Walk 1H 29
SG6: L Gar 3C 16
Greenways SG1: Stev 3G 27
Grenville Way SG2: Stev 2E 31
Gresley Way SG1: Stev 6C 24
SG2: Stev 6G 31
(not continuous)
Greydells Rd. SG1: Stev 2G 27
Griffin Cl. SG4: Hit 2D 20
Grimstone Rd. SG4: L Wym ..3A 22
Grinders End SG4: G'ley 3D 22
Grosvenor Ct. SG2: Stev 2C 26
Grosvenor Rd. SG7: Bald 2D 12
Grosvenor Rd. W. SG7: Bald ..2D 12
Grove Cl. SG15: Arl 2A 4
Grove Ho. SG4: Hit 3E 15
Grovelands Av. SG4: Hit 3F 15
Groveland Way SG5: Stot ...4G 5
Grove Mill Cl. SG4: Hit 3E 15
Grove Rd. SG1: Stev 2E 27
SG4: Hit 5D 14
SG5: Hit 5D 14
Groveside SG16: H'low 1A 2
Guildford Cl. SG1: Stev 5H 23
Gun La. SG3: Kneb 6D 30
Gun Mdw. Av. SG3: Kneb ...6H 31
Gunnels Wood Pk. SG1: Stev ..6F 27
Gunnels Wood Rd.
SG1: Stev 2D 26
Gun Rd. SG3: Kneb 6H 31
Gun Rd. Gdns. SG3: Kneb ...6G 31
Gurney's La. SG5: Hol 4D 8

H

Haddon Cl. SG2: Stev 4G 31
Hadleigh SG6: L Gar 1D 16
Hadrians Wlk. SG1: Stev 1C 28
Hadrian Way SG7: Bald 4B 12
Hadwell Cl. SG2: Stev 6A 28
Half Acre SG5: Hit 1B 20
Hall Mead SG6: L Gar 5C 10
Hallgreen La. SG4: West 2D 24
Hallworth Dr. SG5: Stot 3E 5
Hallworth Ho. SG5: Stot 3E 5
(off Hallworth Dr.)
Halsey Dr. SG4: Hit 6F 15
Halyard Ind. Est. SG6: L Gar ..4H 11
Hambidge Way
SG5: Ick, Pirt 2A 14
(not continuous)
Hammerdell SG6: L Gar 4D 10
Hammond Cl. SG1: Stev 3F 27
Hamonte SG6: L Gar 1E 17
Hampden Cl. SG6: L Gar 3H 11
Hampden Rd. SG4: Hit 4G 15
SG6: L Gar 3H 11
Hampton Cl. SG2: Stev 4G 31
Hanover Cl. SG2: Stev 2D 30
Hardwick Cl. SG2: Stev 4G 31
Hardy Cl. SG4: Hit 6G 15
Harefield SG2: Stev 6C 28
Hare Pk. Ter. SG6: L Sto 6A 2
Harkness Cl. SG4: Hit 4F 15
(off Franklin Gdns.)
Harkness Way SG4: Hit 3G 15
Harper Cl. SG1: Stev 4H 27
Harrier Mill SG16: H'low 1A 2
Harrison Cl. SG4: Hit 6D 14
Harrow Cl. SG1: Stev 4G 27
Harrowdene SG2: Stev 5C 28
Hartland Ct. SG5: Hit 6B 14
Harvest La. SG4: Hit 6D 14
Harvey Rd. SG2: Stev 3B 28
Harwood Pk. Crematorium
SG3: Kneb 5G 31
Haselfoot SG6: L Gar 5E 11
Hastings Cl. SG1: Stev 1C 26
Hatch La. SG4: West 6D 12
Haven, The SG5: Stot 3F 5
Hawkfield SG6: L Gar 3E 11
Hawthorn Cl. SG5: Hit 1B 20
Hawthorn Hill SG6: L Gar ...4E 11
Hawthorns, The SG1: Stev ...5A 28
SG16: H'low 1A 2
Hawthorn Way SG16: L Ston ..1A 8
Haybluff Dr. SG1: West 3A 24

Haycock Round SG1: West ...4A 24
Haycroft Rd. SG1: Stev 2F 27
Hayfield SG2: Stev 2D 28
Haygarth SG3: Kneb 6H 31
Hayley Comn. SG2: Stev 6C 28
Haymoor SG6: L Gar 4E 11
Haysman Cl. SG6: L Gar 4H 11
Hazel Cl. SG4: Hit 6E 15
Hazel Gro. SG5: Stot 4E 5
Hazelmere Rd. SG2: Stev ...3E 31
Hazelwood Cl. SG5: Hit 5D 14
HBS Sports Cen. 6C 14
Headingley Cl. SG1: Stev ...1G 27
Heathcliff Dr. SG5: Stev 1B 10
Heathermere SG6: L Gar 2F 11
Heathfield SG5: Hit 4C 14
Heath Hall SG7: Bald 4D 12
Hedgerow Cl. SG1: Stev 1C 28
Hedgerows, The SG2: Stev ...1D 28
Hellards Rd. SG1: Stev 2F 27
Hellebore Ct. SG1: Stev 1B 28
Hendren Cl. SG1: Stev 6A 24
HENLOW 1A 2
Henlow Greyhound Stadium ...5C 2
Henlow Ind. Est. SG16: H'low ..5D 2
Hensley Cl. SG4: Hit 1F 21
Hermitage, The SG15: Arl ...1B 4
Hermitage Rd. SG5: Hit 6D 14
Herne Rd. SG1: Stev 6D 22
Heron Way SG5: Stot 3E 5
Hertford Ho. SG1: Stev 3D 26
Hertford Rd. SG2: Stev 2D 30
Hibberts Ct. SG6: L Gar 4E 11
HICKMAN'S HILL 2D 18
Higgins Wlk. SG1: Stev 4H 27
High Av. SG6: L Gar 6D 10
Highbury Rd. SG4: Hit 1E 21
Highbush Rd. SG5: Stot 4E 5
Highcroft SG2: Stev 2D 30
High Dane SG6: L Gar 4E 15
Highfield SG6: L Gar 1H 15
Highfield Cl. SG1: Stev 2G 27
Highover Rd. SG6: L Gar 6D 10
Highover Way SG4: Hit 4F 15
High Plash SG1: Stev 4G 27
High St. SG1: Stev 2E 27
SG2: Walk 2H 29
SG4: G'ley 2E 23
SG4: Gos 6C 20
SG5: Hit 6C 14
SG5: Stot 3E 5
SG7: Bald 3D 12
SG15: Arl 3A 4
SG16: H'low 1F 3
High Vw. SG5: Hit 1B 20
Hillary Ri. SG15: Arl 4B 4
Hillbrow SG6: L Gar 6D 10
Hillcrest SG1: Stev 4G 27
SG7: Bald 4D 12
Hillcrest Pk. SG6: L Gar 5B 10
Hillfield Av. SG4: Hit 3E 15
Hillgate SG4: Hit 2E 15
Hillmead SG3: Kneb 3A 28
Hillpath SG6: L Gar 5H 11
Hillshott SG6: L Gar 5G 11
Hillside SG1: Stev 4H 27
Hillside Ho. SG1: Stev 4H 27
Hillside Pk. SG7: Bald 4E 13
Hillside Rd.
SG16: L Ston, U Sto 6A 2
Hilltop SG7: Bald 4C 12
Hilton Cl. SG1: Stev 2D 26
Hine Way SG1: Stev 4A 14
Hinwick Cl. SG15: Arl 2B 4
HITCHIN 6C 14
Hitchin Bus. Cen., The
..........2E 15
Hitchin Cen. Sports Cen. ...5F 15
HITCHIN HILL 2D 20
Hitchin Hill SG4: Hit 1D 20
Hitchin Hill Path SG4: Hit ...2D 20
HITCHIN HOSPITAL
(LABURNUM HOUSE) ...5B 14
Hitchin Mus. & Art Gallery ...6C 14
Hitchin Rd. SG1: Stev 5D 22
SG4: Gos 3D 20
SG4: Gt Wym 1H 21
SG4: West 3G 17
SG5: Stot 1D 10
SG6: L Gar 2A 16
SG15: Arl 6A 4

Hitchin Rd.—Mallard Rd.

Hitchin Rd. SG16: H'low 5D **2**
SG17: Shef 1B **2**
Hitchin Rd. Ind. & Bus. Cen.
SG15: Arl 6H **3**
Hitchin Station (Rail) 5E **15**
Hitchin St. SG7: Bald 3C **12**
Hitchin Swimming Cen. 5C **14**
Hobbs Cl. SG4: St Ipo 6F **21**
Hobbs Ct. SG1: Stev 1A **28**
Holdbrook SG4: Hit 6F **15**
Holden Cl. SG4: Hit 6G **15**
Holders La. SG2: Ast E 4E **29**
Hollow La. SG4: Hit 6D **14**
Holly Copse SG1: Stev 5H **27**
Holly Leys SG2: Stev 3F **31**
Hollyshaws SG2: Stev 1F **31**
Hollywood Bowl
Stevenage 4E **27**
Holmdale SG6: L Gar 6G **11**
Holroyd Cres. SG7: Bald 4C **12**
HOLWELL 4D **8**
Holwell *SG1: Stev 5E 23*
(off Coreys Mill La.)
HOLWELLBURY 1D **8**
Holwell Rd. SG5: Hol 4D **8**
SG5: Pirt 6A **8**
Home Cl. SG5: Stot 3F **5**
Homestead Moat
SG1: Stev 4G **27**
Hopewell Rd. SG7: Bald 3B **12**
Hopton Rd. SG1: Stev 2C **26**
Horace Gay Gdns.
SG6: L Gar 6E **11**
Hornbeam Ct. SG4: Gt Wym 2A **22**
Hornbeams, The SG2: Stev 5B **28**
Hornbeam Spring
SG3: Kneb 6G **31**
Horseshoe Cotts. *SG4: Hit 1D 20*
(off Park St.)
Hospital Rd. SG15: Arl 5H **3**
House La. SG15: Arl 2A **4**
Howard Cl. SG5: Stot 4E **5**
Howard Ct. SG6: L Gar 1D **16**
Howard Dr. SG6: L Gar 2C **16**
Howarde Ct. SG1: Stev 3E **27**
Howard Ga. SG6: L Gar 1D **16**
Howard Pk. Cnr.
SG6: L Gar 5G **11**
Howards Wood SG6: L Gar 2D **16**
Howberry Grn. SG15: Arl 6H **3**
Hudson Rd. SG2: Stev 2B **28**
Humber Ct. SG1: Stev 4H **23**
Hunters Cl. SG2: Stev 2D **28**
SG5: Stot 3E **5**
Hunt Hill Cl. SG1: Stev 4B **24**
Huntingdon Rd. SG1: Stev 1D **26**
Hunting Ga. SG4: Hit 2E **15**
Hurst Cl. SG7: Bald 2E **13**
Hyatt Trad. Est. SG1: Stev 4C **26**
Hyde, The SG2: Stev 6C **28**
Hydean Way SG2: Stev 6A **28**
Hyde Av. SG5: Stot 4E **5**
Hyde Grn. E. SG2: Stev 6B **28**
Hyde Grn. Nth. SG2: Stev 6B **28**
Hyde Grn. Sth. SG2: Stev 6B **28**

I

Ibberson Way SG4: Hit 6E **15**
Iceni Ct. SG6: L Gar 4H **11**
ICKLEFORD 1C **14**
Ickleford *SG1: Stev 5E 23*
(off Coreys Mill La.)
Ickleford Bury SG5: Ick 2C **14**
Ickleford Rd. SG5: Hit 4D **14**
Icknield Cl. SG5: Ick 1C **14**
Icknield Grn. SG6: L Gar 5E **11**
Icknield Way SG6: L Gar 5C **10**
SG7: Bald 2C **12**
Icknield Way E. SG7: Bald 2D **12**
Ingelheim Ct. SG1: Stev 2F **27**
Ingleside Dr. SG1: Stev 5C **22**
Inn's Cl. SG1: Stev 3F **27**
Inskip Cres. SG1: Stev 4G **27**
Iona Cl. SG1: Stev 5H **23**
Iredale Vw. SG7: Bald 2E **13**
Ireton Ct. SG1: Stev 3E **27**
Ivatt Ct. SG4: Hit 6G **15**
Ivel Ct. SG6: L Gar 1E **17**
Ivel Rd. SG1: Stev 2E **27**
Ivel Way SG5: Stot 1F **5**
SG7: Bald 5E **13**

J

Jackdaw Cl. SG2: Stev 5D **28**
Jackman's Pl. SG6: L Gar 5H **11**
Jacks Hill SG4: G'ley 6E **17**
SG6: G'ley 6E **17**
Jacks Hill Pk. SG4: G'ley 6E **17**
Jackson St. SG7: Bald 2C **12**
James Foster Ho. SG5: Hit 4C **14**
James Way SG1: Stev 2E **27**
Jarden SG6: L Gar 1E **17**
Jasmine Ct. SG5: Stot 2F **5**
Jay Cl. SG6: L Gar 3E **11**
Jeeves Yd. SG4: Hit 1D **20**
Jennings Cl. SG1: Stev 6G **27**
Jessop Rd. SG1: Stev 1A **28**
Jeve Cl. SG7: Bald 2E **13**
Jill Grey Pl. SG4: Hit 1D **20**
John Barker Pl. SG5: Hit 4A **14**
John Henry Newman Leisure Cen.
... .6D **22**
John Howland Cl.
SG16: H'low 1F **3**
Jordan Cl. SG16: H'low 1A **2**
Jowitt Ho. SG1: Stev 3G **27**
Jubilee Cl. SG16: H'low 6D **2**
Jubilee Cres. SG15: Arl 1H **9**
Jubilee Memorial Av.
SG1: Stev 1F **27**
(not continuous)
Jubilee Rd. SG1: Stev 1D **26**
SG6: L Gar 4A **12**
Jubilee Trade Cen.
SG6: L Gar 4B **12**
Julia Ga. SG2: Stev 1C **28**
Julian's Cl. SG1: Stev 1E **27**
Julian's Rd. SG1: Stev 1D **26**
Jupiter Ga. SG2: Stev 1D **28**

K

Kardwell Cl. SG4: Hit 1E **21**
Karen Ho. SG16: H'low 5C **2**
Keats Cl. SG2: Stev 2C **28**
Keats Way SG4: Hit 6G **15**
Keiths Wood SG3: Kneb 6D **30**
Keller Cl. SG2: Stev 5B **28**
Kendale Rd. SG4: Hit 1D **20**
Kenilworth Cl. SG2: Stev 4G **31**
Kenmare Cl. SG1: Stev 4H **23**
Kennet Way SG1: Stev 4A **24**
Kent Pl. SG5: Hit 5B **14**
Kerr Cl. SG3: Kneb 6D **30**
Kershaw's Hill SG4: Hit 1D **20**
(not continuous)
Kessingland Av. SG1: Stev 6C **22**
Kestrel Cl. SG2: Stev 1H **31**
Kestrel Wlk. SG6: L Gar 2D **16**
Kilby Rd. SG1: Stev 3E **27**
Kimberley SG6: L Gar 2F **11**
Kimbolton Cres. SG2: Stev 3D **30**
Kimpton *SG1: Stev 5E 23*
(off Coreys Mill La.)
Kingfisher Ct. SG4: Hit 1E **21**
SG6: L Gar 3E **11**
Kingfisher Ri. SG2: Stev 1H **31**
King George Cl. SG1: Stev 3G **27**
King Georges Cl. SG5: Hit 3B **14**
Kings Ct. SG1: Stev 5F **27**
Kingsdown SG4: Hit 1F **21**
Kings Hedges SG5: Hit 4A **14**
(not continuous)
Kingsley Av. SG5: Stot 6C **4**
King's Rd. SG5: Hit 5D **14**
Kings Walden Ri. SG2: Stev 2C **28**
Kings Way SG1: Stev 4E **27**
Kingsway SG5: Stot 2F **5**
Kingsway Gdns. SG5: Stot 2E **5**
Kingswood Av. SG4: Hit 4H **15**
Kipling Cl. SG4: Hit 6G **15**
Kitcheners La. SG2: Walk 6H **25**
Kitchen Garden Ct. SG5: Hit 1C **20**
Kitching La. SG1: Stev 4B **26**
Kite Way SG6: L Gar 3E **11**
Kiwi Ct. SG5: Hit 4D **14**
Knap Cl. SG6: L Gar 3A **12**
KNEBWORTH 6E **31**
Knebworth Country Pk. 4A **30**
Knebworth Ga. SG2: Stev 3D **30**
Knebworth House 5A **30**
Knebworth Station (Rail) 6D **30**
Knights Ct. SG7: Bald 5C **12**
Knights Templars Grn.
SG1: Stev 1C **28**
SG2: Stev 1C **28**
Knights Templar Sports Cen.
... .3C **12**
Knott Cl. SG1: Stev 4B **24**
Knowle SG1: Stev 6D **22**
Knowl Piece SG4: Hit 2E **15**
Kristiansand Way
SG6: L Gar 3A **12**
Kymswell Rd. SG2: Stev 5C **28**
Kyrkeby SG6: L Gar 1E **17**

L

Lacerta Ct. SG6: L Gar 3B **12**
Lacre Way SG6: L Gar 4A **12**
LA Fitness
Stevenage 5F **27**
Lamb Mdw. SG15: Arl 6H **3**
Lammas Mead SG5: Hit 3C **14**
Lammas Path SG2: Stev 5B **28**
Lammas Way SG6: L Gar 3F **11**
Lancaster Av. SG5: Hit 5C **14**
Lancaster Cl. SG1: Stev 5G **23**
Lancaster Rd. SG5: Hit 5C **14**
Langbridge Cl. SG4: Hit 2E **21**
Langleigh SG6: L Gar 2F **11**
Langthorne Av. SG1: Stev 3G **27**
Lannock SG6: L Gar 1F **17**
Lannock Hill SG4: West 3F **17**
SG6: Will 3F **17**
Lanterns SG2: Stev 2C **28**
Lanterns La. SG2: Ast E 3D **28**
Lanthony Ct. SG15: Arl 5A **4**
Lapwing Dell SG6: L Gar 3D **16**
Lapwing Ri. SG2: Stev 6D **28**
Larch Av. SG4: St Ipo 3E **21**
Larkins Cl. SG7: Bald 2D **12**
Larkinson SG1: Stev 2E **27**
Larwood Gro. SG1: Stev 1A **28**
Latchmore Cl. SG4: Hit 2D **20**
Laurel M. SG7: Bald 2D **12**
Laurel Way SG5: Ick 2C **14**
Lavender Ct. SG7: Bald 2C **12**
Lavender Cft. *SG4: Hit 1F 21*
(off Wymondley Rd.)
Lavender Flds. SG5: Hit 6A **14**
Lavender Way SG5: Hit 6B **14**
Lawns, The SG2: Stev 5D **28**
Lawrence Av. SG1: Stev 2G **27**
SG6: L Gar 1C **16**
Lawrence Mead
SG4: L Wym 3B **22**
Laxton Gdns. SG7: Bald 4E **13**
Leas, The SG7: Bald 4C **12**
Leaves Spring SG2: Stev 1D **30**
Leggett Gro. SG1: Stev 1G **27**
Leslie Cl. SG2: Stev 1G **31**
Letchmore Cl. SG1: Stev 3F **27**
Letchmore Rd. SG1: Stev 3F **27**
(not continuous)
Letchworth Bus. & Retail Pk.
SG6: L Gar 4A **12**
LETCHWORTH GARDEN CITY
... .5F **11**
Letchworth Garden City Station (Rail)
... .5F **11**
Letchworth Ga. SG6: L Gar 6H **11**
Letchworth La. SG6: L Gar 2B **16**
Letchworth Mus. & Art Gallery
... .6F **11**
Letchworth Rd. SG7: Bald 4B **12**
Letchworth Shop. Cen.
SG6: L Gar 5F **11**
Letchworth Swimming Pool 4G **11**
Letchworth Tennis Club 2B **16**
Letter Box Row SG4: Gos 4D **20**
Lewis La. SG15: Arl 3A **4**
Leyden Rd. SG1: Stev 6F **27**
Leys Av. SG6: L Gar 5F **11**
Lily Wlk. *SG16: L Ston 6C 2*
(off Orchard Way)
Lime Cl. SG2: Stev 5D **28**
Limekiln La. SG7: Bald 4D **12**
Limes, The SG5: Hit 1B **20**
Lime Wlk. SG16: H'low 1A **2**
Lincoln Rd. SG1: Stev 5B **24**
Lindencroft SG6: L Gar 2G **11**
Lindens, The SG1: Stev 5G **27**
Lindsay Av. SG4: Hit 2F **21**
Lingfield Rd. SG1: Stev 6C **24**
Link, The SG6: L Gar 2G **11**
Linkways Ct. *SG1: Stev 4H 27*
(off Linkways E.)
Linkways E. SG1: Stev 4H **27**
Linkways W. SG1: Stev 4H **27**
Linnet Cl. SG6: L Gar 3E **11**
Linten Cl. SG4: Hit 1G **21**
Lintott Cl. SG1: Stev 3F **27**
Lismore SG2: Stev 2G **31**
Lister Av. SG4: Hit 2D **20**
Lister Cl. SG1: Stev 5E **23**
LISTER HOSPITAL 5D **22**
LITTLE ALMSHOE 6F **21**
Littlebury Cl. SG5: Stot 4G **5**
Little Hyde SG2: Stev 5B **28**
Little La. SG5: Pirt 6A **8**
(not continuous)
LITTLE WYMONDLEY 4A **22**
Lit. Wymondley By-Pass
SG1: Stev 3G **21**
SG4: Hit, L Wym 3G **21**
Livingstone Link SG2: Stev 1B **28**
Lodge Ct. SG5: Ick 2C **14**
Lodge Way SG2: Stev 2E **31**
Lolleywood La. SG4: West 5F **19**
Lomond Way SG1: Stev 5C **24**
London Rd. SG1: Stev 5F **27**
SG2: Stev 5F **27**
SG3: Kneb 6E **31**
SG4: Hit, St Ipo ... .2D **20** & 5A **26**
SG7: Bald 5D **12**
(not continuous)
London Row SG15: Arl 6A **4**
Long Cl. SG16: L Ston 1A **8**
Longcroft Rd. SG1: Stev 2G **27**
Longfield SG1: Stev 1D **26**
Longfield Ct. SG6: L Gar 4D **10**
Longfields SG2: Stev 2G **31**
Long Hyde SG2: Stev 5B **28**
Long La. SG2: Ast E 4D **28**
Long Leaves SG2: Stev 1E **31**
Longmead SG6: L Gar 4E **11**
Longmeadow Dr. SG5: Ick 6G **9**
Longmeadow Grn.
SG2: Stev 2G **31**
Long Ridge SG2: A'ton 2H **31**
Lonsdale Ct. SG1: Stev 2H **27**
Lonsdale Rd. SG1: Stev 1H **27**
Lordship Cen. SG6: L Gar 2C **16**
Lordship Cotts. SG6: Will 3D **16**
Lordship La. SG6: L Gar 1D **16**
Lovell Cl. SG4: Hit 1E **21**
LOWER GREEN 6H **9**
Lower Innings SG5: Hit 5B **14**
Lower Sean SG2: Stev 6A **28**
LOWER STONDON 6B **2**
LOWER TITMORE GREEN 6B **22**
Lowes Cl. SG1: Stev 5C **24**
Lucas La. SG5: Hit 5B **14**
Lygrave SG2: Stev 3G **31**
Lyle's Row SG4: Hit 1D **20**
Lymans Rd. SG15: Arl 3A **4**
Lymington Rd. SG1: Stev 1D **26**
Lyndale SG1: Stev 5G **27**
Lynton Av. SG15: Arl 4A **4**
Lytton Av. SG6: L Gar 6F **1**
Lytton Flds. SG3: Kneb 6D **3**
Lytton Way SG1: Stev 2E **27**

M

Macfadyen Webb Ho.
SG6: L Gar 4G **1**
Mackenzie Sq. SG2: Stev 6B **2**
Maddles SG6: L Gar 1F **1**
Made Feld SG1: Stev 4H **2**
Magdalene Ct. *SG7: Bald 2D 1*
(off Royston Rd
Magellan Cl. SG2: Stev 4D **2**
Magpie Cres. SG2: Stev 5D **2**
Maiden St. SG4: West 4B **1**
Mallard Rd. SG2: Stev 1H **3**

36 A-Z Stevenage

Malthouse La.—Park Pl. Chambers

Malthouse La. SG5: Stot 2G 5
Maltings, The SG2: Walk 1H 29
SG6: Nort 2A 12
SG16: H'low 2A 2
Maltings Cl. SG7: Bald 2E 13
Malvern Cl. SG2: Stev 4F 31
Manchester Cl. SG1: Stev 4H 23
Mandeville SG2: Stev 3G 31
Manor Cl. SG5: Ick 2C 14
SG6: L Gar 2B 16
Manor Cotts. SG6: L Gar 3D 16
Manor Cres. SG4: Hit 1F 21
Manor Farm SG16: U Sto 5A 2
Mnr. Farm Stables
SG3: Old K 6A 30
Manor Ho. Dr. SG2: Stev 2D 28
Manor Rd. SG16: H'low 2A 2
Manor Vw. SG2: Stev 2F 31
Manor Way SG6: L Gar 2B 16
Mansfield M. *SG7: Bald 3D 12*
(off Mansfield Rd.)
Mansfield Rd. SG7: Bald 4C 12
Manton Rd. SG4: Hit 1F 21
Maple Cl. SG16: L Ston 1A 8
Maples, The SG2: Stev 2F 31
SG4: Hit 2D 20
Maples Ct. SG5: Hit 6C 14
Marcus Cl. SG1: Stev 1C 28
Market Pl. SG1: Stev 4F 27
SG5: Hit 6C 14
Market Sq. SG1: Stev 4F 27
Marlborough Cl. SG4: West . . .5B 18
Marlborough Rd. SG2: Stev . . .4C 28
Marlowe Cl. SG2: Stev 1C 28
Marmet Av. SG6: L Gar 5E 11
Marquis Bus. Cen.
SG7: Bald 2E 13
Marriotts Gymnastics Cen. . . .3A 28
Marschefield SG5: Stot 3E 5
Marshgate SG1: Stev 4F 27
Martin's Ho. SG1: Stev 6A 24
Martins Way SG1: Stev 1E 27
Martin Way SG6: L Gar 6D 10
Marymead Ct. SG2: Stev 3E 31
Marymead Dr. SG2: Stev 3E 31
Marymead Ind. Est.
SG2: Stev 3E 31
Masefield SG4: Hit 6G 15
Mathews Cl. SG1: Stev 6F 23
Matthew Ga. SG4: Hit 2E 21
Mattocke Rd. SG5: Hit 4A 14
Maxwell Rd. SG1: Stev 4D 26
Maxwell's Path SG5: Hit 5B 14
Maycroft SG6: L Gar 2G 11
Maydencroft La. SG4: Gos 3B 20
Mayfield Cres. SG16: L Ston 1A 8
Mayles Cl. SG1: Stev 2D 26
Maylin Cl. SG4: Hit 5G 15
Maytrees SG4: Hit 1E 21
Mead, The SG5: Hit 3C 14
Mead Cl. SG1: Stev 3H 27
Meadow Bank SG4: Hit 5F 15
Meadowsweet SG16: L Ston 1B 8
Meadow Wlk. SG16: H'low 1F 3
Meadow Way SG1: Stev 4H 27
SG5: Hit 1B 20
SG5: Stot 3F 5
SG6: L Gar 6F 11
Meads, The SG6: L Gar 5E 11
Meadway SG1: Stev 3D 26
(Gunnels Wood Rd.)
SG1: Stev 3C 26
(Redcar Dr.)
SG3: Kneb 6G 31
Meadway Ct. SG1: Stev 3D 26
Meadway Technical Pk.
SG1: Stev 3C 26
Mecca Bingo Club
Stevenage 4F 27
Medalls Link SG2: Stev 6A 28
Medalls Path SG2: Stev 6A 28
Meeting Ho. La. SG7: Bald 2C 12
Melbourne Cl. SG5: Stot 3F 5
Melne Rd. SG2: Stev 3F 31
Mendip Way SG1: Stev 4A 24
SG1: West 3B 24
Meppershall Rd. SG16: U Sto . . .5A 2
Merchants Wlk. SG7: Bald 2F 13
Mercia Rd. SG7: Bald 3E 13
Meredews SG6: L Gar 4H 11
Meredith Rd. SG1: Stev 1A 28
Mermaid Cl. SG4: Hit 6F 15
Merrick Cl. SG1: West 3B 24
Mews, The SG6: Nort 2A 12
Michael Muir Ho. SG5: Hit 4B 14
Middlefield La. SG16: H'low 2E 3
Middlefields SG6: L Gar 2F 11
Middlefields Ct. *SG6: L Gar 2F 11*
(off Middlefields)
Middle Row SG1: Stev 2E 27
Middlesborough Cl.
SG1: Stev 5H 23
Middlesex Ho. SG1: Stev 3D 26
Midhurst SG6: L Gar 3F 11
Midland Cotts. SG5: Hit 4E 15
Midland Way SG16: H'low 6D 2
Mildmay Rd. SG1: Stev 1B 28
Milestone Cl. SG2: Stev 5D 28
Milestone Rd. SG3: Kneb 6E 31
SG5: Hit 4B 14
Milksey La. SG4: G'ley 2E 23
Millard Way SG4: Hit 3G 15
Mill Cl. SG4: Hit 5G 15
SG5: Stot 3G 5
SG16: H'low 1A 2
Miller Ho. Rd. SG1: Stev 3G 27
Millfield La. SG4: St Ipo 3D 20
Mill La. SG4: Gos, St Ipo 4D 20
SG4: West 4C 18
SG5: Stot 3G 5
SG15: Arl 6H 3
Mill Rd. SG4: St Ipo 4D 20
Millstream Cl. SG4: Hit 3D 14
Mill Way SG5: Ick 2A 14
Millwood Ct. SG5: Stot 3F 5
Milne Cl. SG6: L Gar 2D 16
Milton Vw. SG4: Hit 6G 15
Mindenhall Ct. *SG1: Stev 2E 27*
(off High St.)
Minehead Way SG1: Stev 2C 26
Minerva Cl. SG2: Stev 6C 24
Minsden Rd. SG2: Stev 6D 28
Mixies, The SG5: Stot 3E 5
Mobbsbury Way SG2: Stev 2B 28
Monklands SG6: L Gar 5D 10
Monks Cl. SG6: L Gar 5C 10
Monks Vw. SG2: Stev 1D 30
Monkswood Retail Pk.
SG1: Stev 6G 27
Monkswood Way SG1: Stev . . .5G 27
SG2: Stev 1C 30
Mons Av. SG7: Bald 5D 12
Montfitchet Wlk. SG2: Stev 1D 28
Moormead Cl. SG5: Hit 1B 20
Moormead Hill SG5: Hit 1A 20
Moors Ley SG2: Walk 6G 25
Morecambe Cl. SG1: Stev 2D 26
Morello Gdns. SG4: Hit 2E 21
Morgan Cl. SG1: Stev 6F 23
Morris Cl. SG16: H'low 4E 3
Moss Way SG5: Hit 4A 14
Mt. Garrison SG4: Hit 6D 14
Mountjoy SG4: Hit 4G 15
Mount Keen SG1: West 4C 24
Mt. Pleasant SG5: Hit 1B 20
Mowbray Cres. SG5: Stot 3F 5
Mowbray Gdns. SG4: Hit 2E 21
Mowbrays, The SG5: Stot 2F 5
Mozart Ct. SG1: Stev 4E 27
Muddy La. SG6: L Gar 2B 16
Muirhead Way SG3: Kneb 6D 30
Mulberry Cl. SG5: Stot 4F 5
Mulberry Way SG5: Hit 3B 14
Mullway SG6: L Gar 5C 10
Mundesley Cl. SG1: Stev 6D 22
Muntings, The SG2: Stev 6A 28
Munts Mdw. SG4: West 4C 18
Murrell La. SG5: Stot 4G 5
Myrtle Gdns. SG16: L Ston 6C 2

N

Narrowbox La. SG2: Stev 2C 28
Nash Cl. SG2: Stev 3B 28
Neagh Cl. SG1: Stev 4C 24
Nene Rd. SG16: H'low 5D 2
Neptune Ga. SG2: Stev 6D 24
Netherstones SG5: Stot 2F 5
Netley Dell SG6: L Gar 2D 16
Nevell's Grn. SG6: L Gar 4F 11
Nevells Rd. SG6: L Gar 5F 11
Nevilles Ct. SG6: L Gar 3A 12
Nevis Rd. SG1: West 3A 24
Newbury Cl. SG1: Stev 6F 23
Newcastle Cl. SG1: Stev 4H 23
New Cl. SG3: Kneb 5D 30
Newells SG6: L Gar 1E 17
Newells Way SG6: L Gar 6B 12
New England Cl.
SG4: St Ipo 3D 20
Newgate SG2: Stev 5A 28
Newhaven SG2: Stev 2B 28
Newlands SG6: L Gar 2C 16
Newlands Cl. E. SG4: Hit 3D 20
Newlands Cl. W. SG4: Hit 3D 20
Newlands La. SG4: Hit 3D 20
Newlyn Cl. SG1: Stev 3C 26
NEWNHAM 2D 6
Newnham Hall 1D 6
Newnham Rd.
SG7: New, R'well 2D 6
New Rd. SG17: Clift 1C 2
Newton Rd. SG2: Stev 3B 28
Newtons Way SG4: Hit 1D 20
Newtown SG16: H'low 1A 2
Nicholas Pl. SG1: Stev 6F 23
Nickleby Way SG5: L Gar 1C 10
Nightingale Ct. SG5: Hit 5E 15
Nightingale Rd. SG5: Hit 5D 14
Nightingale Ter. SG15: Arl 6A 4
Nightingale Wlk. SG2: Stev 4C 28
Nightingale Way SG7: Bald 5C 12
Nimbus Way SG4: Hit 6G 15
Ninesprings Way SG4: Hit 1F 21
Nodes Dr. SG2: Stev 2E 31
Noke, The SG2: Stev 3F 31
Nokeside SG2: Stev 3F 31
Normans Cl. SG6: L Gar 2F 11
North Av. SG6: L Gar 3H 11
Northern Av. SG16: H'low 6D 2
Northfield Cl. SG16: H'low 1A 2
Northfields SG6: L Gar 2F 11
Northgate SG1: Stev 4F 27
North Herts Leisure Cen. 5A 12
North Pl. SG5: Hit 4B 14
North Rd. SG1: Stev 4E 23
SG4: Stev 4E 23
NORTON 2A 12
Norton Bury La. SG6: Nort 1A 12
Norton Cres. SG7: Bald 3C 12
NORTON GREEN 6D 26
Norton Grn. Rd. SG1: Stev 5E 27
Norton Mill La. SG6: Nort 6B 6
SG7: Bald 6B 6
Norton Rd. SG1: Stev 5F 27
SG5: Nort, Stot 5G 5
SG6: L Gar, Nort 3G 11
SG6: Nort 5G 5
SG7: Bald 1A 12
Norton Way Nth. SG6: L Gar . . .5G 11
Norton Way Sth. SG6: L Gar . . .5G 11
Norwich Cl. SG1: Stev 6B 24
Nun's Cl. SG5: Hit 6C 14
NUP END GREEN 6A 30
Nursery Cl. SG2: Stev 3E 31
Nursery Ct. SG6: L Gar 5F 11
Nursery Hill SG4: Hit 1D 20
Nutleigh Gro. SG5: Hit 4B 14

O

Oak Dr. SG16: H'low 2A 2
OAKFIELD 1E 21
Oakfield Av. SG4: Hit 2F 21
Oakfields SG2: Stev 2F 31
Oakfields Av. SG3: Kneb 5E 31
Oakfields Cl. SG2: Stev 2G 31
Oakfields Rd. SG3: Kneb 5E 31
Oakhill SG6: L Gar 1F 17
Oak La. SG4: G'ley 3D 22
Oaks Cl. SG4: Hit 2D 20
Oaks Cross SG2: Stev 2F 31
Oaktree Cl. SG6: L Gar 1A 16
Oakwell Cl. SG2: Stev 4H 31
Oakwood Cl. SG2: Stev 1G 31
Offley Rd. SG5: Hit 1B 20
Old Bakery SG5: Hit 6C 14
Old Barn Cl. SG16: H'low 1A 2
Old Bourne Way SG1: Stev 4A 24
Old Brewery Cl. SG5: Stot 2F 5
Old Chantry SG1: Stev 5C 22
Old Charlton Rd. SG5: Hit 1C 20
Olden Mead SG6: L Gar 2D 16
Olde Swan Ct. SG1: Stev 2E 27
Oldfield Farm Rd.
SG16: H'low 5D 2
(not continuous)
Old Hale Way SG5: Hit 4C 14
OLD KNEBWORTH 5A 30
Old Knebworth La.
SG1: Stev 5A 30
SG2: Stev 5A 30
SG3: Kneb, Old K 5A 30
Old La. SG3: Kneb 6E 31
Old Oak Cl. SG15: Arl 1A 4
Old Oak Ind. Est. SG15: Arl 1H 3
Old Park Rd. SG5: Hit 6C 14
Old School Wlk. SG15: Arl 5A 4
OLD STEVENAGE 2E 27
Old Vicarage Gdns.
SG16: H'low 1A 2
Old Walled Garden, The
SG1: Stev 6E 23
Oliver's La. SG5: Stot 2F 5
Olympus Rd. SG16: H'low 5D 2
Openshaw Way SG6: L Gar 5F 11
Orchard, The SG7: Bald 3D 12
Orchard Cl. SG4: St Ipo 4D 20
SG6: L Gar 3F 11
Orchard Cres. SG1: Stev 2E 27
Orchard Ho. SG6: L Gar 3F 11
Orchard Rd. SG1: Stev 2E 27
SG4: Hit 4F 15
SG7: Bald 2C 12
Orchard Vw. SG4: Hit 4F 15
Orchard Way SG3: Kneb 6C 30
SG6: L Gar 3F 11
SG16: L Ston 1C 8
Ordelmere SG6: L Gar 2F 11
Orion Ga. SG1: Stev 4H 27
Orlando Cl. SG4: Hit 1E 21
Orwell Av. SG1: Stev 4H 23
Orwell Vw. SG7: Bald 2F 13
Osbourne Ct. SG7: Bald 4D 12
Osier Ct. SG5: Hit 5D 14
Osprey Ct. SG6: L Gar 3E 11
Osprey Gdns. SG2: Stev 1H 31
Osterley Cl. SG2: Stev 4G 31
Oughton Cl. SG5: Hit 5B 14
Oughton Head La. SG5: Hit 5A 14
(not continuous)
Oughton Head Way SG5: Hit . . .5B 14
Oundle, The SG2: Stev 2G 31
Oundle Ct. SG2: Stev 3G 31
Oundle Path SG2: Stev 3G 31
Oval, The SG1: Stev 6A 24
SG16: H'low 6E 3
Owen Jones Cl. SG16: H'low 4E 3
Oxleys Rd. SG2: Stev 6B 28

P

Pacatian Way SG1: Stev 1C 28
Paddock, The SG4: Hit 2E 21
Paddock Cl. SG6: L Gar 6G 11
Paddocks, The SG2: Stev 5B 28
Paddocks Cl. SG2: Stev 5B 28
Page Cl. SG7: Bald 5D 12
Palmerston Ct. SG2: Stev 2B 28
Palmerston Way SG5: Stot 1C 10
Pankhurst Cres. SG2: Stev 4C 28
Parade, The *SG6: L Gar 2F 11*
(off Southfields)
Parishes Mead SG2: Stev 5D 28
Park Cl. SG2: Stev 2F 31
SG7: Bald 4C 12
Park Ct. SG6: L Gar 5G 11
Park Cres. SG7: Bald 4C 12
Park Dr. SG7: Bald 4C 12
Parker Cl. SG6: L Gar 1A 16
Parker's Fld. SG2: Stev 5C 28
Park Farm Cl. SG16: H'low 1F 3
Parkfield SG6: L Gar 1F 17
Park Gdns. SG7: Bald 4C 12
Park Ga. SG4: Hit 1D 20
Park La. SG3: Old K 6A 30
SG16: H'low 1A 2
Park La. Cres. SG16: H'low 1A 2
Park Pl. SG1: Stev 4F 27
Park Pl. Chambers
SG1: Stev 4F 27

A-Z Stevenage 37

Park St. SG4: Hit 1C 20
SG7: Bald 3C 12
Park Vw. SG2: Stev 2F 31
Park Way SG4: Hit 1C 20
SG5: Hit 1C 20
Parkway SG2: Stev 2E 31
Parsons Grn. Ind. Est.
SG1: Stev 5C 24
Pascal Way SG6: L Gar 3H 11
Passingham Av. SG4: Hit 1E 21
Pasture Rd. SG6: L Gar 2A 16
Pastures, The SG2: Stev 1D 28
SG16: U Sto 6A 2
Paxton Dr. SG5: L Gar 1C 10
Paynes Cl. SG6: L Gar 2G 11
Payne's Pk. SG5: Hit 6C 14
Pearl Ct. SG7: Bald 3D 12
Pearsall Cl. SG6: L Gar 6H 11
Pear Tree Cl. SG16: L Ston 6D 2
Pear Tree Dell SG6: L Gar 2D 16
Peartree Way SG2: Stev 6A 28
Pebbles, The SG7: R'well 5A 6
Peckworth Ind. Est.
SG16: L Ston 5C 2
Pelican Way SG6: L Gar 2F 11
Pembroke Rd. SG7: Bald 3D 12
Penfold Cl. SG7: Bald 4E 13
Pennine Ct. SG5: Hit 5C 14
Penn Rd. SG1: Stev 4G 27
Penn Way SG6: L Gar 2D 16
Pentland Ri. SG1: Stev 4C 24
Pepper All. SG7: Bald 3D 12
Peppercorn Wlk. SG4: Hit 6F 15
Pepper Ct. SG7: Bald 3C 12
Peppermint Rd. SG5: Hit 6D 14
Pepsal End SG2: Stev 3F 31
Pepys Way SG7: Bald 3C 12
Periwinkle La. SG5: Hit 4D 14
Peters Way SG3: Kneb 5D 30
Petworth Cl. SG2: Stev 4G 31
Pike End SG1: Stev 3F 27
Pilgrims Way SG1: Stev 6A 24
PINEHILL PRIVATE HOSPITAL 6F 15
Pinetree Ct. SG1: Stev 5F 27
Pinewoods SG2: Stev 2D 30
PIN GREEN 1A 28
Pin Grn. Ind. Est. SG1: Stev 5B 24
(not continuous)
Pinnocks Cl. SG7: Bald 4D 12
Pinnocks La. SG7: Bald 4D 12
PIRTON 6A 8
Pirton Cl. SG5: Hit 6B 14
Pirton Rd. SG5: Hit 1A 20
SG5: Hol 5C 8
Pitt Ct. SG2: Stev 2F 31
Pix Brook Ct. SG6: L Gar 4F 11
Pix Ct. SG15: Arl 1A 4
Pixmore Av. SG6: L Gar 5H 11
Pixmore Cen. SG6: L Gar 5G 11
Pixmore Ind. Est. SG6: L Gar 5G 11
Pixmore Way SG6: L Gar 6F 11
Pix Rd. SG5: Stot 4E 5
SG6: L Gar 5G 11
Plash Dr. SG1: Stev 4G 27
Plinston Hall 6F 11
Plum Tree Rd. SG16: L Ston 6D 2
Pollard Gdns. SG1: Stev 1H 27
Pollards Way SG16: L Ston 1C 8
Pond Cl. SG1: Stev 2E 27
Pondcroft Rd. SG3: Kneb 6E 31
Pond La. SG7: Bald 3C 12
Pondside SG4: G'ley 3E 23
Poplar Cl. SG4: Hit 1E 21
Poplar Dr. SG5: Stot 1F 5
POPLARS 6C 28
Poplars, The SG5: Ick 5H 9
SG15: Arl 1A 4
Popple Way SG1: Stev 3G 27
Poppy Mead SG1: Stev 5H 27
Portland Ind. Est. SG15: Arl 1H 9
Portman Cl. SG5: Hit 3B 14
Portmill La. SG5: Hit 6D 14
Post Office Row SG4: West 4B 18
Potters La. SG1: Stev 5D 26
Pound Av. SG1: Stev 3F 27
Pound Ct. SG1: Stev 3F 27
Prestatyn Cl. SG1: Stev 2D 26
Preston Rd. SG4: Gos, Pres 5D 20
Priestley Rd. SG2: Stev 4B 28
Primary Way SG15: Arl 5A 4
Primett Rd. SG1: Stev 2E 27
Primrose Cl. SG15: Arl 5H 3
Primrose Ct. SG1: Stev 2F 27
Primrose Hill Rd. SG1: Stev 2F 27
Primrose La. SG15: Arl 5H 3
Prince Andrew Dr. SG5: Stot 3G 5
Prince Charles Av. SG5: Stot 3G 5
Prince Edward Way SG5: Stot 3G 5
Prince Harry Cl. SG5: Stot 3G 5
Prince of Wales Cl. SG15: Arl 6A 4
Prince's St. SG5: Stot 2F 5
Prince William Cl. SG5: Stot 4G 5
Principal Ct. SG6: L Gar 3G 11
Priory Ct. SG4: Hit 2D 20
Priory Dell SG1: Stev 4G 27
Priory End SG4: Hit 1D 20
Priory La. SG4: L Wym 3B 22
Priory Vw. SG4: L Wym 3A 22
Priory Way SG4: Hit 3C 20
Protea Ind. Est. SG6: L Gar 5H 11
Protea Way SG6: L Gar 5H 11
Providence Ct. SG7: Bald 4D 12
Providence Gro. SG1: Stev 1G 27
Providence Way SG7: Bald 4D 12
Pryor Ct. SG1: Stev 2F 27
Pryor Gdns. SG5: Stot 2F 5
Pryor Rd. SG7: Bald 4D 12
Pryors Ct. *SG7: Bald 2D 12*
(off Clothall Rd.)
Pryors Wood Nature Reserve 6D 24
Pryor Way SG6: L Gar 1F 17
Pullman Dr. SG4: Hit 6F 15
Pulter's Way SG4: Hit 1E 21
Purcell Ct. SG1: Stev 1E 27
PURWELL 4G 15
Purwell La. SG4: Hit 5G 15
Pyms Cl. SG6: L Gar 3H 11

Q

Quadrant, The SG1: Stev 5F 27
SG6: L Gar 5F 11
Quantock Cl. SG1: West 4D 24
Queen Anne's Cl. SG5: Stot 4F 5
Queen Mother Theatre 6D 14
Queen St. SG4: Hit 1D 20
SG5: Stot 4G 5
Queensway SG1: Stev 4F 27
Queenswood Dr. SG4: Hit 4G 15
Quills SG6: L Gar 1F 17
Quinn Way SG6: L Gar 6A 12

R

Raban Cl. SG2: Stev 2G 31
Raban Ct. SG7: Bald 2D 12
Radburn Cnr. SG6: L Gar 6A 12
Radburn Way SG6: L Gar 1D 16
Radcliffe Rd. SG5: Hit 5E 15
RADWELL 5A 6
Radwell Cotts. SG7: R'well 5A 6
Radwell La. SG7: R'well 5A 6
Railway, The SG16: H'low 6D 2
Raleigh Cres. SG2: Stev 1A 28
Rally, The SG15: Arl 2A 4
(not continuous)
Ralph Swingler Pl.
SG6: L Gar 1B 16
Ramerick Gdns. SG15: Arl 1H 9
Ramsdell SG1: Stev 4H 27
Ram Yd. SG15: Arl 5A 4
Randalls Hill SG2: Stev 6B 28
Rand's Cl. SG5: Hol 4D 8
Rand's Mdw. SG5: Hol 4D 8
Ransom Cl. SG4: Hit 3D 20
Ransom's Yd. SG5: Hit 6D 14
Ranworth Av. SG2: Stev 4G 31
Rectory Cft. SG1: Stev 6F 23
Rectory Farm Bus. Pk.
SG16: U Sto 6A 2
Rectory La. SG1: Stev 6E 23
Redcar Dr. SG1: Stev 3C 26
REDCOTES GREEN 5H 21
Redhill Rd. SG5: Hit 5A 14
Redhoods Way E.
SG6: L Gar 4E 11
Redhoods Way W.
SG6: L Gar 5E 11
Redoubt Cl. SG4: Hit 4E 15
Redwing Cl. SG2: Stev 5C 28
Regal Ct. SG5: Hit 5D 14
Regency Ct. Pk. Homes
SG16: L Ston 1A 8
Regent Ct. SG5: Stot 2F 5
Regent St. SG5: Stot 3E 5
Reynolds SG6: L Gar 2F 11
Rhee Spring SG7: Bald 2F 13
Riccat La. SG1: Stev 4H 23
Rickyard, The SG6: Nort 2A 12
Riddell Gdns. SG7: Bald 3D 12
Riddy Hill Cl. SG4: Hit 1E 21
Riddy La. SG4: Hit 1E 21
Ridge, The SG6: L Gar 5G 11
Ridge Av. SG6: L Gar 5G 11
Ridge Rd. SG6: L Gar 5G 11
Ridgeway SG1: Stev 4H 27
Ridgeway, The SG5: Hit 1B 20
Ridings, The SG2: Stev 6B 28
Ridlins End SG2: Stev 1G 31
Ringtale Pl. SG7: Bald 2F 13
Ripon Rd. SG1: Stev 5H 23
Rise, The SG7: Bald 4C 12
Riverain Bowls Club 4E 15
River Ct. SG5: Ick 1D 14
River Mead SG5: Hit 3A 14
Rivett Cl. SG7: Bald 2E 13
Roaring Meg Retail & Leisure Pk.
SG1: Stev 6G 27
Robert Ellis Ct. SG3: Kneb 6E 31
Robert Humbert Ho.
SG6: L Gar 6G 11
Robert Saunders Ct.
SG6: L Gar 1A 16
Robert Tebbutt Ct. SG5: Hit 6C 14
Robins Hill SG4: Hit 1D 20
Rockingham Way SG1: Stev 6G 27
Roebuck Ct. SG2: Stev 2D 30
Roebuck Ga. SG2: Stev 2D 30
Roebuck Retail Pk.
SG2: Stev 1C 30
Roe Cl. SG5: Stot 4E 5
Roman La. SG7: Bald 3D 12
Romany Cl. SG6: L Gar 5C 10
Rookery Cl. SG2: Walk 1H 29
Rookes Cl. SG6: L Gar 2D 16
Rook Tree Cl. SG5: Stot 3G 5
Rook Tree La. SG5: Stot 2F 5
Rookwood Dr. SG2: Stev 2F 31
Rooky Yd. SG1: Stev 2E 27
Rose Cott. Gdns. SG4: Hit 5E 15
Rose Cotts. SG15: Arl 3A 4
Rosemary La. SG16: L Ston 6C 2
Rosemary Lodge *SG5: Hit 6D 14*
(off Whinbush Rd.)
Rosemont Cl. SG6: L Gar 5E 11
Ross Ct. SG2: Stev 2B 28
Round Mead SG2: Stev 6D 28
Roundwood Cl. SG4: Hit 3G 15
Rowan Cl. SG4: West 5B 18
Rowan Cres. SG1: Stev 2F 27
SG6: L Gar 4E 11
Rowan Gro. SG4: St Ipo 3E 21
Rowans, The SG7: Bald 4C 12
Rowland Rd. SG1: Stev 5H 27
Rowland Way SG6: L Gar 5F 11
Roxley Ct. SG6: Will 5D 16
Roxley Mnr. SG6: Will 5D 16
Royal Oak La. SG5: Pirt 6A 8
Royston Rd. SG7: Bald 2D 12
SG7: Byg 1H 13
Ruckles Cl. SG1: Stev 4G 27
Rudd Cl. SG2: Stev 6B 28
Rudham Gro. SG6: L Gar 2E 17
Rundells SG6: L Gar 1F 17
Runnalow SG6: L Gar 4D 10
Runswick Ct. SG1: Stev 2C 26
Rusbridge Ct. *SG7: Bald 2C 12*
(off Football Cl.)
Rushby Mead SG6: L Gar 5G 11
Rushby Pl. SG6: L Gar 6G 11
Rushby Wlk. SG6: L Gar 5G 11
RUSH GREEN 5A 26
Ruskin La. SG4: Hit 6G 15
Russell Cl. SG2: Stev 1F 31
Russell's Slip SG5: Hit 1B 20
Russell Wlk. SG5: Stot 1D 10
Rutherford Cl. SG1: Stev 3C 26
Ryder Av. SG5: Ick 2B 14
Ryders Hill SG1: Stev 4C 24
Ryder Way SG5: Ick 2B 14
Rye Cl. SG1: Stev 4H 23
Ryecroft SG1: Stev 2G 27
Rye Gdns. SG7: Bald 2F 13
Ryley Cl. SG16: H'low 5D 2

S

Sacombe M. SG2: Stev 4H 31
Saddlers Cl. *SG7: Bald 3C 12*
(off Hitchin St.)
Saffron Cl. SG15: Arl 2A 4
Saffron Hill SG6: L Gar 5E 11
St Albans Dr. SG1: Stev 6G 23
St Albans Highway
SG4: Gos, Pres 6D 20
St Albans Link SG1: Stev 6G 23
St Andrews Dr. SG1: Stev 5H 23
St Andrew's Pl. SG4: Hit 6D 14
St Annes Ct. SG5: Hit 5D 14
St Anne's Rd. SG5: Hit 5D 14
St Augustine Cl. SG5: Hit 5D 14
St Davids Cl. SG1: Stev 4H 23
St Elmo Ct. SG4: Hit 2D 20
St Faiths Cl. SG4: Hit 4F 15
St George's Way SG1: Stev 4F 27
ST IBBS 5F 21
ST IPPOLLYTTS 4G 21
ST IPPOLYTS 4G 21
St John's Path SG4: Hit 2D 20
St John's Rd. SG4: Hit 2D 20
SG15: Arl 5A 4
St Katharines Cl. SG5: Ick 2B 14
St Margarets SG2: Stev 1D 30
St Mark's Cl. SG5: Hit 4B 14
St Martin's Rd. SG3: Kneb 6E 31
St Mary's Av. SG5: Stot 3F 5
St Mary's Cl. SG2: A'ton 1H 31
SG6: L Gar 3B 16
St Mary's Way SG7: Bald 5C 12
St Michaels Ct. SG1: Stev 1B 28
St Michael's Mt. SG4: Hit 5E 15
St Michaels Rd. SG4: Hit 5F 15
St Olives SG5: Stot 3E 5
St Pauls Ct. SG2: Stev 2D 30
St Peter's Av. SG15: Arl 2A 4
St Peters Grn. SG5: Hol 4D 8
Sale Dr. SG7: Bald 2D 12
Salisbury Cl. SG5: Stot 1D 10
Salisbury Rd. SG1: Stev 5A 24
SG7: Bald 2C 12
Sanderling Cl. SG6: L Gar 3E 11
Sanders Pl. SG4: Hit 5E 15
Sandover Cl. SG4: Hit 1F 21
Sandown Rd. SG1: Stev 6C 24
Sandy Gro. SG4: Hit 1D 20
Sanfoine Cl. SG4: Hit 5G 15
Saunders Cl. SG6: L Gar 4A 12
Sax Ho. SG6: L Gar 2E 11
Saxon Av. SG5: Stot 1F 5
Saxon Cl. SG6: L Gar 2F 11
Saxon Ct. SG4: Hit 6D 14
Saxon Way SG7: Bald 2F 13
Sayer Way SG3: Kneb 6G 31
Scarborough Av. SG1: Stev 1C 26
School Cl. SG2: Stev 6B 28
Schoolfields SG6: L Gar 6A 12
School La. SG2: A'ton 6E 29
SG4: West 4C 18
School Wlk. SG6: L Gar 5H 11
Scott Rd. SG2: Stev 3B 28
Second Av. SG6: L Gar 5A 12
Seebohm Cl. SG5: Hit 4A 14
Sefton Rd. SG1: Stev 6B 24
Senate Pl. SG1: Stev 4B 24
Serpentine Cl. SG1: Stev 5C 24
Severn Way SG1: Stev 4H 23
Seymour Ct. SG5: Hit 5D 14
Shackledell SG2: Stev 1D 30
Shackleton Spring
SG2: Stev 6A 28
Shaftesbury Ct. SG1: Stev 5G 27
Shaftesbury Dr. SG5: Stot 6C 4
Shaftesbury Ind. Cen.
SG6: L Gar 4G 11
Shannon Cl. SG16: L Ston 1A 8
Sharps Ct. SG4: Hit 4E 15
Sharps Way SG4: Hit 4E 15
Sheafgreen La. SG2: Ast E 4D 28
SG2: Stev 4D 28

Shearwater Cl. SG2: Stev 5D 28
Sheepcroft Hill SG2: Stev 6D 28
Shelley Cl. SG4: Hit 6G 15
SHEPHALL **6A 28**
Shephall Grn. SG2: Stev 1E 31
Shephall Grn La. SG2: Stev . . .1F 31
Shephall La. SG2: Stev 2D 30
      (not continuous)
Shephall Leisure Cen. 1F 31
Shephall Vw. SG1: Stev 4A 28
Shephall Way SG1: Stev 5B 28
Shepherds La. SG1: Stev 3B 26
Shepherds Mead SG5: Hit 3C 14
Sheringham Av. SG1: Stev 6D 22
Sherwood SG6: L Gar 3F 11
Shillington Rd. SG16: L Ston 1A 8
Shire Cl. SG1: Stev 2E 27
Shirley Cl. SG2: Stev 1B 28
Shoreham Cl. SG1: Stev 1C 26
Short La. SG2: Ast E 5E 29
Shott La. SG6: L Gar 5G 11
Siccut Rd. SG4: L Wym 3A 22
Siddons Rd. SG2: Stev 3C 28
Sidings, The SG16: H'low 6D 2
Signal Cl. SG16: H'low 6D 2
Silam Rd. SG1: Stev 4G 27
Silkin Cl. SG2: Stev 6D 28
Silkin Way SG1: Stev 4F 27
Silverbirch Av. SG5: Stot 1F 5
Silver Cl. SG5: Hit 5C 14
Simpson Dr. SG7: Bald 3D 12
Simpsons Cl. SG7: Bald 3D 12
Sinfield Cl. SG1: Stev 4A 28
Sish Cl. SG1: Stev 3F 27
      (not continuous)
Sish La. SG1: Stev 3F 27
Sisson Cl. SG2: Stev 1G 31
Six Hills Way SG1: Stev 6E 27
SG2: Stev 5G 27
Sixth Av. SG6: L Gar 5A 12
Skegness Rd. SG1: Stev 1C 26
Skipton Cl. SG2: Stev 3D 30
Skylark Cnr. SG2: Stev 6D 28
Sleaps Hyde SG2: Stev 2G 31
Slip La. SG3: Old K 6A 30
Sloan Cl. SG1: Stev 3H 27
SNAILSWELL **6G 9**
Snailswell La. SG5: Ick 6G 9
Snipe, The SG4: West 4B 18
Snowdonia Way SG1: West 3A 24
Sollershott E. SG6: L Gar 1B 16
Sollershott Hall SG6: L Gar 1B 16
Sollershott W. SG6: L Gar 1A 16
Sorrel Gth. SG4: Hit 1E 21
Souberie Av. SG6: L Gar 6F 11
South Cl. SG7: Bald 4D 12
Southend Cl. SG1: Stev 2F 27
Southern Av. SG16: H'low 6D 2
Southern Way SG1: Stev 2E 11
Southfields SG6: L Gar 2F 11
Southgate SG1: Stev 5F 27
      (not continuous)
South Hill Cl. SG4: Hit 1E 21
Sth. Lodge M. SG7: Bald 4D 12
South Pl. SG5: Hit 5B 14
South Rd. SG7: Bald 4D 12
Southsea Rd. SG1: Stev 1D 26
South Vw. SG6: L Gar 6F 11
Southwark Cl. SG1: Stev 6B 24
Southwold Cl. SG2: Stev 3C 26
Sparhawke SG6: L Gar 2G 11
Sparksfield SG16: H'low 1A 2
Sparrow Dr. SG2: Stev 5D 28
Speke Cl. SG2: Stev 4D 28
Spellbrooke SG5: Hit 5B 14
Spencer Way SG6: L Gar 3F 11
Sperberry Hill SG4: St Ipo 5F 21
Spinney, The SG2: Stev 2D 28
SG7: Bald 4C 12
Spinney Cl. SG4: Hit 1F 21
Spreckley Cl. SG16: H'low 4D 2
Spring Dr. SG2: Stev 3E 31
Spring Rd. SG6: L Gar 5E 11
      (not continuous)
Springshott SG6: L Gar 6E 11
Spur, The SG1: Stev 5G 27
Spurrs Cl. SG4: Hit 6F 15
Standalone Farm Cen. 3D 10
Standhill Cl. SG4: Hit 1D 20
Standhill Rd. SG4: Hit 1D 20
Stane Fld. SG6: L Gar 2D 16

Stane St. SG7: Bald 2E 13
Stanley Rd. SG2: Stev 1B 28
Stanmore Rd. SG1: Stev 2F 27
Starlings Bri. SG5: Hit 5D 14
Station App. SG3: Kneb 6D 30
SG4: Hit 5E 15
Station Cl. SG16: H'low 6D 2
Station Pde. SG6: L Gar 5F 11
      (off Station Rd.)
Station Pl. SG6: L Gar 5F 11
Station Rd. SG3: Kneb 6D 30
SG6: L Gar 5F 11
SG7: Bald 2D 12
SG15: Arl 5A 4
SG16: L Ston 1A 8
Station Ter. SG4: Hit 5E 15
Station Way SG6: L Gar 5E 11
Stephenson M. SG2: Stev 5B 28
Stephenson Wlk. SG5: L Gar . . .1C 10
Sterling Ct. SG1: Stev 5F 27
STEVENAGE **4F 27**
Stevenage Arts & Leisure Cen.
   . . . . .4F 27
Stevenage Arts Society
   (Springfield House) 2E 27
Stevenage Borough FC
   (Stevenage Stadium) 1C 30
Stevenage Borough Football Academy
   . . . . .1E 31
Stevenage Bus. & Ind. Pk.
   . . . . .5C 24
STEVENAGE CYGNET HOSPITAL
   . . . . .5D 22
Stevenage Ent. Cen.
   SG1: Stev 2D 26
Stevenage Leisure Pk.
   SG1: Stev 5E 27
Stevenage Mus. 4G 27
Stevenage Rd.
   SG2: Stev, Walk 1E 29
   SG3: Kneb 3D 30
   SG4: Hit, L Wym 2D 20
   SG4: L Wym, St Ipo 4F 21
Stevenage Station (Rail) 4E 27
Stevenage Swimming Cen. 4G 27
Stirling Cl. SG2: Stev 4H 31
SG4: Hit 6G 15
Stobarts Cl. SG3: Kneb 5D 30
Stockbridge Rd. SG16: H'low . . .1A 2
Stockens Dell SG3: Kneb 6G 31
Stockens Grn. SG3: Kneb 6G 31
Stondon Transport Mus. 6B 2
Stonecroft SG3: Kneb 6D 30
Stoneley SG6: L Gar 2F 11
Stonnells Cl. SG6: L Gar 3F 11
Stony Cft. SG1: Stev 3G 27
Storehouse La. SG4: Hit 1D 20
Stormont Rd. SG5: Hit 4D 14
STOTFOLD **3E 5**
STOTFOLD GREEN **1F 5**
Stotfold Rd. SG4: Hit 5C 10
SG6: L Gar 4C 10
      (not continuous)
SG7: Cald 1H 5
SG15: Arl 1A 4
Strafford Ct. SG3: Kneb 6E 31
Strathmore Av. SG5: Hit 4C 14
Strathmore Cl. SG5: Hit 4D 14
Straw Plait Way SG15: Arl 5H 3
Stuart Dr. SG4: Hit 6F 15
Sturgeon Rd. SG4: Hit 3F 15
Sturgeon's Way SG4: Hit 3F 15
Sturrock Way SG4: Hit 1G 21
Such Cl. SG6: L Gar 4H 11
Summerfield Ct. SG5: Stot 3E 5
SUNNYSIDE **2E 21**
Sunnyside Rd. SG4: Hit 2E 21
Sun St. SG5: Hit 1C 14
SG7: Bald 3C 12
Super Karts Indoor Karting Cen.
   . . . . .5H 11
      (off Pixmore Av.)
Sutcliffe Cl. SG1: Stev 1A 28
Swale Cl. SG1: Stev 4A 24
Swangley's La. SG3: Kneb 6E 31
Swanstand SG1: Stev 1F 17
Sweyns Mead SG2: Stev 2C 28
Swift Cl. SG6: L Gar 3E 11
Swinburne Av. SG5: Hit 4A 14
Swingate SG1: Stev 4F 27
Sycamore Cl. SG4: St Ipo 3E 21

Sycamores, The SG7: Bald 3C 12
SYMONDS GREEN **3C 26**
Symonds Grn. La. SG1: Stev . . .3C 26
Symonds Grn. Rd.
   SG1: Stev 2C 26
      (not continuous)
Symonds Rd. SG5: Hit 5B 14

Y

SAFETY CAMERA INFORMATION

Safety camera locations are publicised by the Safer Roads Partnership who operate them in order to encourage driver's to comply with speed limits at these sites. It is the driver's absolute responsibility to be aware of and to adhere to speed limits at all times.

By showing this safety camera information it is the intention of Geographers' A-Z Map Company Ltd., to encourage safe driving and greater awareness of speed limits and vehicle speed. Data accurate at time of printing.